STEEL
AND
ECONOMIC GROWTH
IN MEXICO

Latin American Monographs, No. 7
Institute of Latin American Studies
The University of Texas

STEEL
AND
ECONOMIC GROWTH
IN MEXICO

by William E. Cole

Published for the INSTITUTE OF LATIN AMERICAN STUDIES
by the UNIVERSITY OF TEXAS PRESS, Austin & London

Library of Congress Catalog Card No. 67–19285
Copyright © 1967 by William E. Cole
All Rights Reserved

Printed in the United States of America
by the Printing Division of The University of Texas, Austin
Bound by Universal Bookbindery, Inc., San Antonio

Acknowledgments

A special debt of gratitude is owed to Professor Wendell C. Gordon, who as a teacher stimulated the author's interests in Latin American economic problems, and a special word of thanks is extended to Professor Eastin Nelson for introducing the author to the panorama of the Mexican economy. I am also indebted to Professor Siegfried Garbuny for reading the manuscript and making many useful suggestions.

I wish also to thank those who worked so capably with various stages of the manuscript: Mrs. Ralph Krug, Letitia McCann, and Martha Teffeteller.

W. E. C.

Knoxville, Tennessee

Contents

Tables

Figures

Introduction

This study has a twofold purpose: first, to present an industry study of iron and steel in Mexico and, second, to make some attempts to assess the impact of that industry upon some other sectors of the economy. Concomitant with both of these themes will be an analysis of the role of the Mexican government in promoting and regulating the steel industry. This will entail a description of Mexico's policy of infant industry protection and import substitution.

The technology for producing iron came relatively late to Mexico, arriving with the Spanish Conquistadores. Until the twentieth century the mining of ore and the forging of the metal was done in small-scale enterprises that served to fill local needs. By the turn of the century the railroad grid had come to link Mexico's diverse regions and Porfirio Díaz had used his personal power to subject state and regional leaders to control by the central government, thus eliminating interstate tariff barriers to trade. These two occurrences, the railroad and political unification, acted to give Mexico an embryo national market. In response, private capital, for the most part foreign, founded Latin America's first integrated steel mill in Monterrey. In addition to furnishing the transportation necessary for a national market, the railroads were consumers of much of the new steel mill's output, which was limited to finished products such as rails and construction rods that required no further milling. Transformation industries were few and far between, which meant that the markets for such products as steel plate, sheet steel, and tin plate were almost nonexistent.

The "second epoch" of Mexico's steel industry began in the early 1940's, when World War II brought a boom in Mexican exports which, coupled with curtailed world supplies of steel, created a situation that to the Mexican government seemed ripe for the expansion of existing steel capacity. As will be noted in Chapters 1 and 2, the Mexican government through direct investment, and acting as a financial intermediary, provided for the establishment of new capacity, and through the implementation of tariff barriers protected that industry from competition. Taking into consideration the political atmosphere that called for import replacement, we will evaluate in Chapter 3 the efficiency of the measures used to promote that policy, not the efficacy of the policy itself. Judgment of the policy decision would require a study of possible alternatives that were open to the Mexican government and comparison of probable results from alternative investments and promotions with the results achieved in fact in the steel industry. Such evaluations are outside the scope of this study.

The cost data used to quantify the conceptual tools of Chapters 3 and 4 and Appendix A are taken from the United Nations' *A Study of the Iron and Steel Industry in Latin America* (1957). The data have two shortcomings which may lead to questions as to their suitability to our purposes. First, the data are hypothetical, and, second, they are based on factor costs at 1948 prices. The data are based on a hypothetical plant located in Monclova but the processes employed in this model are very similar to those in use in the actual Monclova mill, and costs of the various inputs were derived from the Mexican experience. While the unit cost of steel production has changed since 1948 and the factor proportions may well have changed, nevertheless the magnitude of economies of scale likely remain a function of plant size, as was the case with the hypothetical 1948 data. This general relationship is all that the data are intended to show. In no sense are the figures intended to be taken as precise measurements of economies of scale. While the conceptual tools developed in Chapters 3 and 4 do not enable us to measure the impact of import substitution on the economy, hopefully they do enable us to take a more refined look at the nature of foreign exchange savings derived from an import substitution policy and the nature of price effects of such a policy.

Chapter 3 makes the point that the backward linkage "pull" of a steel industry may result in imports of raw materials. Where reserves of a basic raw material are nonexistent, increased demand for that input can be satisfied only through imports, with consequent outlays in foreign exchange.

Chapter 4 endeavors to point out that with steel available from domestic suppliers, the enforcement of an import substitution policy may have some deleterious effects upon steel consumption if domestic costs are higher than world prices. While Hirschman[1] assigns a high degree of forward linkage "push" effect to the establishment of a steel industry, he has not explicitly considered that the push effect of higher priced domestic steel might be less than that of lower priced imports. Certainly adverse price effects should not be taken as precluding establishment of a domestic industry, but although we cannot isolate the microprice effects from the general equilibrium considerations brought about by the establishment of the industry, we should not assume that the mere existence of a domestic steel supply is going to induce increased use of steel as inputs by other industries.

Chapter 5 presents a study of production and consumption of steel both in aggregate terms and broken down by product. Chapter 6 presents an analysis of steel consumption by consuming sector and then presents projections of steel consumption both by product type and consuming sector. These projections indicate a healthy future for the industry.

A steel industry is said to exercise a backward linkage inducement for domestic provision of inputs. According to Hirschman,[2] iron and steel have a high degree of interdependence through purchases from other sectors. True, the interdependence exists, but the effectiveness of the backward pull depends upon the existence of domestic reserves of the raw materials used as inputs as well as the existence of capital goods industries. In the absence of domestic reserves of raw materials, the backward pull of the steel industry can result in increased imports. Chapter 7 describes in detail the Mexican situation regarding the steel industry's basic raw materials and also some of the satellite industries built up in conjunction with the coking process. Both ore and coal are available in Mexico, but one basic raw material in short supply in Mexico is scrap, and the backward linkage pull of increased steel production has called for increased imports of that item, as detailed in Chapters 7 and 8.

Chapter 8 deals with Mexican foreign trade in iron and steel products. Detailed data on a product basis are presented for both imports and exports, and import data based on country of origin are also presented.

Woven throughout most of the following pages is the history of

[1] Albert O. Hirschman, *The Strategy of Economic Development*, p. 106.
[2] *Ibid.*

the development of the Mexican steel industry and interspersed at various points are attempts to assess the impact of that industry upon some of the sectors of Mexico's economy. Much space is also devoted to the role of the Mexican federal government in the promotion of the industry.

In all instances where the words *ton* or *tons* appear, reference is to the metric ton, which is the equivalent of 2,204.6 pounds (1,000 kilograms).

STEEL
AND
ECONOMIC GROWTH
IN MEXICO

1. History of
Iron and Steel in Mexico

Iron ore is widely distributed over the face of the earth and is found in mixture with rock or earth. The ore is made up of the pure metal (Fe) in combination with oxygen, carbon, and sulphur. The amount of each of these substances varies in the various ores of the earth, and other substances may appear with these basic ones. Heat in sufficient quantities will separate some of the impurities or nonmetallic substances from the iron, leaving a more or less crude metal. It would seem to have been inevitable that primitive man, by using rock and earth as building materials, eventually would have placed ore-bearing rock or earth in some fortuitous and juxtaposed combination with fire and wind so that sufficient heat would be present to reduce the ore to a metal. By some "combination of accident and intuition" the process of smelting iron was discovered in the Middle East more than one thousand years before the time of Christ, and the knowledge of the process was communicated to Egypt and the Aegean.[1]

A commonplace today, a workhorse when compared to such thoroughbred ores as gold and silver, or even copper, iron was rare and often precious to early man. In ancient Athens in Odyssean times, iron was used in the giving of gifts and as treasure or store of value.[2] As iron became more ordinary, its uses became more varied. The use of iron and iron technology pushed slowly northward, reaching the upper Danube about 900 B.C.[3] The Celts, in their migrations, brought it to France and the Iberian Peninsula on the west and to Germany and the British Isles on the north.

[1] Norman G. Pounds, *Geography of Iron and Steel*, p. 11.
[2] Moses Finley, *The World of Odysseus*, pp. 51–52.
[3] Pounds, *Geography of Iron and Steel*, p. 11.

In those early times the primitive technique for mining the ores consisted of collecting or scraping them from outcrops on the surface.[4] As mentioned earlier, iron ore is not found in a state of pure metal, but is mixed with earthen and/or stony material. This extraneous material is given the technical name of *gangue*. Primitive methods for removing the gangue included washing and pounding. When the gangue was less dense and when it had a stony quality, the technique of pounding with hammers was employed to remove the impurities.[5]

The primitive fuel used to smelt the ores was charcoal made from wood or peat. Coke was to enter the scene much later. The technique of making charcoal was developed in ancient times and the method "described by Aristotle's disciple Theophrastus . . . has remained essentially unaltered."[6] This dependence on supplies of wood dictated the location of the iron-working furnaces just as today the location of coking coal dictates the location of the steel mills.

Archaeological evidence is clear that the aborigines of Mexico had developed a technology of metallurgy prior to the coming of the Spanish; however, while the evidence shows that the Indians both smelted and forged gold, silver, copper, tin, bronze, and lead, it indicates that they probably had no knowledge of iron.[7] The sequence of use followed that which occurred in the Middle East and Europe, where the Bronze Age preceded the Iron Age. The Indians of Mexico had learned to work with the many indigenous metals that have relatively low melting points, but the potential usefulness of iron ore that was everywhere in abundance had not been conceived. They fashioned many artifacts, such as jewelry of gold, and axes of bronze,[8] but it is not possible to determine whether the bronze was alloyed from separate ores of copper and tin or from an ore containing elements of both metals. However, it is known that the Aztecs fashioned objects constituted of alloys of gold, silver, and copper and also alloys of copper and lead.[9]

Methods of mining and smelting were primitive, with gold being mined by individuals "panning" with their hands in the rivers. In actuality, very little is known about the methods of extraction used

[4] H. R. Schubert, *History of the British Iron and Steel Industry*, p. 4.
[5] *Ibid.*, p. 17
[6] *Ibid.*, p. 18.
[7] Modesto Bargallo, *La Minería y la Metalurgía*, p. 25.
[8] *Ibid.*, p. 26.
[9] *Ibid.*, p. 28.

either by the early aborigines or in times more recent to the Conquest. Early Spanish arrivals in New Spain saw Indians smelting gold in small pans using tubes of cane as bellows to elevate the temperature produced by the fire; however, in Peru, Bolivia, Ecuador, and Chile the Indians had fashioned intricate smelting furnaces called *guarias* in which they smelted silver and copper.[10] But, as in Mexico, none of the civilizations indigenous to the Americas seems to have worked with iron prior to the arrival of the Spanish.

Although archeological evidence indicates a long history of metal-working on a very small scale, it would probably be proper to date the beginning of the minerals industry in Mexico near the middle of the sixteenth century. Jenaro González, in assigning this date refers to the development of the industry on a grand scale:

. . . [d]el siglo XVI, cuando el espíritu de adventura y sed de riqueza incitaron a los españoles a emprender sus notables viajes y exploraciones a través de la Nueva España, en busca de minas.[11]

On his second voyage to the New World, Columbus brought 1,590 men, among whom were many miners whose job was to mine gold ore.[12] None of this group was bound for Mexico; however, after Cortez spoke to Charles V of the golden treasures of Montezuma, expeditions were dispatched to Mexico also. In 1526 Cortez sent an expedition to what is now the state of Oaxaca to take possession of the rich gold deposits. Very shortly thereafter the copper and tin in Tlacho and the silver in Taxco were exploited by the Spaniards.

The Conquistadores discovered the famous Cerro de Mercado in the state of Durango in the year 1552. The discovery was made by one Ginés Vásquez de Mercado who led an expedition north from Guadalajara "in search of a legendary mountain of gold and silver."[13] When he brought his expedition upon what was reputed to be the legendary mountain, he found to his great disappointment that there was iron everywhere and no sign of the precious metals. Returning without success, his band was almost annihilated by the Tepehuan Indians. The dying Vásquez de Mercado is reputed to

---

[10] *Ibid.*, p. 40.
[11] Jenaro González, *Riqueza Minera y Yacimientos Minerales de México*, p. 1.
[12] Bargallo, *La Minería y la Metalurgía*, p. 48.
[13] Pablo Sada, "Some Notes on the Organization of the Monclova Steel Works," in United Nations, *A Study of the Iron and Steel Industry in Latin America*, II, 337.

have said, "Iron, iron, that is what we need; gold and silver conquered with iron."[14]

The historians and chroniclers of the Mexican colonial period say little or nothing of iron mining or of the iron industry.[15] It is known that some who lived in the vicinity of the Cerro de Mercado smelted the iron ore on a small scale to make agricultural equipment and mining tools. Such smelting operations on a very minor scale were located in other areas of Mexico as well, and always they were designed to satisfy local needs. The method of smelting was by the Catalan forge, a technique imported from Spain where this forge had originated in the province of Catalonia. The first Spanish iron workers to come to New Spain settled in the vicinity of Puebla and at first they used metal from Spain upon which they performed shaping and casting operations.[16]

For the first several decades of the nineteenth century the siderurgical industry remained bound up in small ironworking shops located, as they had been for close to three centuries, near the iron ore deposits. A preponderance of these iron-craft shops was located in the states of Durango, Hidalgo, Jalisco, México, and Oaxaca.[17] In the state of Durango, at the foot of Cerro de Mercado, several small but modern-appearing ironworking operations were set up. Sooner or later, for various reasons, they all failed.

The first of the modern mines for processing iron ore was established in 1828 by the governor of Durango and was called La Ferrería. An accompanying smelting operation established there three years later was called Piedras Azules. This iron smelter utilized the Catalan forge. Production reached as high as five thousand kilograms per week and used fifty thousand pounds of fuel.[18] In 1835 a plant for the production of iron was established at Guadalupe de Zimapan in the state of Hidalgo, a state noted for its mining. The plant was of small scale, and the market for its output was local in scope.[19]

Later, North American capitalists purchased Cerro de Mercado

[14] *Ibid.*
[15] Bargallo, *La Minería y la Metalurgia*, p. 66.
[16] *Ibid.*
[17] *Ibid.*, p. 251.
[18] *Ibid.*, p. 356.
[19] United Nations, *An Inquiry into the Iron and Steel Industry of Mexico*, p. 11.

and in 1881 established an iron smelter under the name of the Iron Mountain Company. This company utilized fairly modern techniques of ore reduction.[20] Other, and yet smaller, operations had been springing up about the country.

It is generally stated, with disregard to the small-scale operations mentioned in the foregoing, that the Mexican iron and steel industry was born in 1900, with the establishment of the Compañía Fundidora de Fierro y Acero de Monterrey, S.A. (hereafter referred to as Fundidora). But at least three other iron smelting or foundry establishments had preceded Fundidora in Monterrey. In 1889 a foundry was established and operated for only a few years. In 1890 Compañía Fundidora y Afinadora de Monterrey, S.A. was founded. Originally owned by Mexican citizens, this company was later acquired by Americans and is still in operation today under the name of Compañía Minera de Peñoles, S.A. But all of the operations that preceded Fundidora were small and none of them approached even the pretense of being an integrated steel mill.

Although La Consolidada, S.A., a company very much in existence today, was also established in 1900, Fundidora was the first integrated iron and steel mill, not only in Mexico but in all of Latin America. "Integrated" in this connection means that in addition to the production of pig iron in blast furnaces, the mill also produces steel from its own "pig" and then rolls the steel into finished products. La Consolidada did not have a blast furnace, and Fundidora remained the only Mexican producer of pig iron until 1944.

The original capacity of Fundidora was 90,000 tons annually. The equipment included a blast furnace with a capacity of 300 tons per day, three Siemens-Martin open-hearth furnaces with a daily steel-making capacity of 35 tons each, a battery of forty-eight beehive ovens for making coke, a 2-high rolling mill for reducing steel ingots, and a mill for making structural shapes and rails.[21] The original investment was ten million pesos derived from investors in France, Italy, and the United States; however, today almost all shares are domestically held.[22] The blast furnace was installed during the period 1901–1903 by William Todd and Company of the

[20] Bargallo, *La Minería y la Metalurgia*, p. 356.
[21] Luis Torón Villegas, *La Industria Siderúrgica Pesada del Norte del México*, p. 55.
[22] Juan Checa de Codes, *La Industria Siderúrgica en Hispanoamérica*, p. 98.

United States, and except for the shutdown of 1913–1915, the mill was in normal operation until 1944.[23] During the period 1941–1943 a new blast furnace with a capacity of 600 tons per day was constructed.[24] This furnace was fired on July 8, 1943, during inaugural ceremonies led by President Avila Camacho.[25] The furnace, a modern American type (refractory lining covered with a metal housing), was constructed entirely in Mexico with as few imported parts as possible.[26] In 1944 operation of the old blast furnace was curtailed drastically, and in 1949 it was closed down.[27] It was closed down because of lack of railcars to haul raw materials and lack of capacity of the steel furnaces to utilize liquid pig iron from both the old and new blast furnaces. Later it was put back into use as the steel-making facilities were expanded and the shortage of railcars abated. Now in operation, its capacity has been increased to 350 tons per day.

The laminating operations at Fundidora were progressively improved to the point that in 1955 there was installed a combination rolling mill capable of fabricating a great variety of products and replacing outdated 11-inch, 12-inch, and 19-inch mills.[28] In 1957 Fundidora initiated a new expansion program which was expected to raise the productive capacity to one million tons per year upon its completion in 1965.[29] Recent production data for Fundidora are shown in Table 1.

It will be noted that the ratio of pig iron production to steel output has varied, especially after 1948. This is probably due to the variations in the proportions of pig iron and scrap metal which are combined inputs for the open-hearth steel furnaces of Fundidora.

It has been argued that the stimulus which motivated the private investment in Fundidora at the turn of the century came from the establishment of a railroad system, the initial link of which was the line from Mexico City to Veracruz that was completed in 1883.

Although the iron and steel products used in the initial construction and operation of the railways, from rails and spikes to wagons and

---

[23] Alejandro A. González, *Un Estudio en la Cía. Fundidora de Fierro y Acero de Monterrey, S.A.*, pp. 122–123.
[24] Torón Villegas, *La Industria Siderúrgica Pesada,*
[25] González, *Un Estudio*, p. 123.
[26] *Ibid.*
[27] *Ibid.*, pp. 122–123.
[28] Torón Villegas, *La Industria Siderúrgica Pesada*, p. 55.
[29] *Ibid.*

TABLE 1

Production of Iron and Steel by La Fundidora de Fierro y Acero
de Monterrey (1944–1960)
(Metric Tons)

Year	Pig Iron	Steel Ingots
1944	135,157	127,485
1945	162,894	142,281
1946	167,524	144,591
1947	172,820	134,986
1948	115,792	117,583
1949	132,875	147,508
1950	118,981	138,938
1951	148,762	158,696
1952	184,992	178,480
1953	126,247	137,002
1954	114,686	145,766
1955	137,612	160,844
1956	174,976	179,447
1957	185,951	210,791
1958	172,074	202,304
1959	179,079	205,421
1960	160,559	220,000

Source: Carlos A. Rivera Rangel, "La Siderúrgica y la Integración Industrial de México," pp. 29–31.

locomotives, were imported, the building of the railways provided the basis for the establishment of a modern large-scale iron and steel industry. Besides stimulation of foreign trade and production, expanding the domestic market, the railways themselves became a good market for iron and steel products. In addition, large-scale production of coal, essential as a fuel in iron and steel production, was stimulated.[30]

If the railway system furnished impetus for the establishment of the steel industry, then the oil industry, which was beginning operations on a large scale, furnished impetus for the expansion of production with its demand for pipe and drill rigs. By 1911 steel production had jumped to 72,000 tons from a base of 11,000 tons in 1903, the year that La Fundidora began production.[31]

[30] United Nations, *An Inquiry into the Iron and Steel Industry of Mexico*, p. 11.
[31] *Ibid.*

Carlos Prieto, president of Fundidora, tells that a major problem in the very early days was the creation of a sufficient market for the products that the mills had capacity to produce.[32] Of course there was, at that time, consumption of modern iron and steel products, but most of that demand was satisfied by imports. The new steel mills hoped to substitute their manufactures for those then imported and to enjoy a substantial share of an expanding market. The management of the steel companies could not have hoped to capture very quickly all of the market provided by domestic steel consumption. In those areas where the final processing of the iron or steel product could be done by the steel mill itself, it could have been hoped that domestic manufactures would substitute for imports; however, where further processing was required beyond the confines of the steel mill, there was less hope for import substitution. The problem, of course, was that Mexico had very few if any factories for transforming the finished steel, such as plate, sheet, and bar, into finished products. For this reason it would be many decades before sheet and plate would be produced.

Although the volume of steel production rose by more than 600 per cent between 1903 and 1911, it was brought to a complete standstill in 1914, as a result of the violence and disruptions of the Revolution. Steel production resumed in 1915, but it was not until 1923 that the tonnage produced was equal to the 72,000 tons produced in 1911. Another sharp decline in production began in 1924, but this time recuperation was more rapid and by 1930 production had reached 89,000 tons.[33]

The world depression of the 1930's, with its drastic diminution in demand, had its adverse effect on Mexican steel production and, although production continued to grow during this period, the rate of growth was greatly diminished. The steel industry in Mexico remained relatively small and insignificant until the 1940's, when World War II brought about worldwide steel shortages with consequent increases in the price of steel. With the advent of the War, the search for markets ended and the iron and steel industries of the world were faced with greatly increased demand as steel marched, flew, and sailed to war.

[32] Carlos Prieto, "La Industria Siderúrgia," *México, 50 Años de Revolución,* I: *La Economía,* 216.

[33] United Nations, *An Inquiry into the Iron and Steel Industry of Mexico,* p. 11.

Carlos Prieto refers to the year 1941 as the beginning of the second epoch of Mexico's iron and steel industry because during that year plans were initiated for the expansion of Fundidora and for the establishment of Altos Hornos de México, S.A. The Spanish phrase *altos hornos* translates into English as "blast furnace," but is a literal translation of the German word *hochoefen*. Hereafter reference to this company will be by its initials: AHMSA, an abbreviation generally used in Mexico which can be pronounced as a word by using the broad "a" of the Spanish alphabet. Also, as previously mentioned, in 1942 Fundidora began construction of a second blast furnace. At the same time it expanded its steel-making capacity by installing new Siemens-Martin steel-making furnaces.[34] But the truly memorable event was the establishment of AHMSA.

AHMSA is located in the city of Monclova in the state of Coahuila. Not only was AHMSA's the second blast furnace to go into operation in Mexico, it was also Latin America's second, and AHMSA was the second integrated steel mill to be established in Latin America. It was a job of combined government and private promotion, with part of the financing being furnished by private sources and part by public. The original investment was financed by the Nacional Financiera, S.A., which is the government's entrepreneurial arm, the Export-Import Bank, the American Rolling Mills Company, and private domestic investors.[35] Private Mexican investors subscribed to 90 per cent of the company's common stock and American Rolling mills took the remaining 10 per cent. Nacional Financiera subscribed to all of the preferred stock, which totaled 26.1 per cent of the total equity of 22,310,000 pesos.[36] Further, Nacional Financiera took on the job of selling 30 million pesos' worth of long-term bonds.

The original plans that culminated in the construction of AHMSA were relatively inauspicious. The plans, as originally drawn up by a group of private financiers, called for a rolling mill of small capacity that would produce flat rolled products. This mill would use imported semifinished steel as its major raw material. However, fear of dependence on foreign sources for raw materials led to abandonment of this scheme and to considerations of an inte-

---

[34] Prieto, "La Industria Siderúrgica," p. 217.
[35] Checa de Codes, *La Industria Siderúrgica en Hispanoamérica*, p. 98.
[36] Wolfgang Friedmann and G. Kalmanoff, *Joint International Business Ventures*, p. 282.

grated operation to use Mexican iron ore and coal.[37] It was because the new project would require a much greater investment that the government stepped in. Nacional Financiera took on the task of mobilizing investment funds.

In December, 1941, AHMSA was officially established with a capitalization of 52,310,000 pesos.[38] Usually such a new venture would entail the purchase and installation of new equipment designed specifically for the new plant, but because of the effects of World War II, new equipment was rarely available. The Mexican promoters were left with two possibilities: one, they could delay the project until the cessation of hostilities or, second, they could attempt to locate used equipment in the hope of commencing production sooner. The latter course was chosen,[39] because, in addition to its scarcity, prices on new mill equipment were skyrocketing by 1941.[40] Thus, not only would used equipment allow an earlier installation, but it would cut the cost of financing the venture.

By such an ignominious birth the giant of Mexico's steel industry was fashioned from bits and pieces found in various parts of the United States. An old blast furnace was located in St. Louis, a universal plate mill was purchased from Youngstown Sheet and Tube Company, and a crane with a 65-ton capacity was purchased from Lukens Steel Company in Coatesville, Pennsylvania.[41] The blast furnace had been closed down shortly after World War I and sold as scrap, and many of its parts required rebuilding and repair.[42]

The universal mill was purchased at a price that amounted to less than the cost of a similar tonnage of scrap iron, but it had to be retooled to make it adaptable to AHMSA's desired output.[43]

AHMSA was able to purchase highly restricted items in the United States because the War Production Board gave them the necessary priority rating.[44] In return for the priority rating, it was agreed that upon completion the company would supply steel plate for shipbuilding to support the United States' war effort.[45]

[37] H. R. Pape, "Five Years of Achievement at Altos Hornos Steel Company," *Basic Industries in Texas and Northern Mexico*, p. 51.
[38] Sada, "Some Notes on Monclova Steel Works," p. 339.
[39] *Ibid.*
[40] Pape, "Five Years of Achievement," p. 53.
[41] *Ibid.*, pp. 54–55.
[42] *Ibid.*, p. 54.
[43] *Ibid.*, p. 55.
[44] *Ibid.*, p. 56.
[45] Sada, "Some Notes on Monclova Steel Works," p. 339.

TABLE 2

Consumption of Steel Products in Mexico by
Secondary Industries in 1949

Consuming Area	Sheet	%	Tons Plate	%	Tin Plate	%
Federal District	6,501	10.07	1,350	8.84	11,097	65.08
Monterrey	19,573	30.31	165	1.08	4,019	23.57
Tlalnepantla	7,219	11.18	12,669	82.98	....	....
Other	31,281	48.44	1,084	7.10	1,936	11.35
Total	64,574	100.00	15,268	100.00	17,052	100.00

Source: Marcelo G. Aramburu, "Consumption of Iron and Steel Products in Mexico," in United Nations, *A Study of the Iron and Steel Industry in Latin America*, p. 440.

Contrary to the expectations of many individuals, Altos Hornos was completed in time and offered and shipped many thousands of tons of ship plate against orders of the Maritime Commission in Washington.[46]

As would be expected, the question of location of the new steel company was deliberated. Deposits of iron ore exist in various areas of Mexico, but coking coal was available only in the north in the Sabinas fields of Coahuila. Besides the location of iron ore and coal, the other factor to be considered was the location of the market. The breakdown of this market as it appeared in 1949 is shown in Table 2.

As will be noted, a large portion of the market is divided between the Monterrey area and the Federal District which meant that a plant located in the vicinity of one market would be far from the other.

Table 3 shows how AHMSA's share of national steel consumption was distributed by locale in 1955. Almost 50 per cent of total sales were made in the Federal District and the State of Mexico. If market orientation were the dominant criterion in locating a steel mill it would appear that AHMSA should have been located near the Federal District. But, following the classical rule of location theory, ore was moved to coal and the location of the market given only secondary consideration. The general rule is that ore is moved to coal because for every ton of steel produced, several tons of coal

[46] Pape, "Five Years of Achievement," p. 58.

TABLE 3

Distribution of AHMSA Sales by States in 1955
(Per Cent)

State	Plate	Sheet	Tinplate	Pipe	Total
Federal District	36.2	52.6	51.7	4.0	43.69
State of México	5.5	8.1	....	0.3	5.66
Coahuila	27.8	9.5	....	....	15.07
Nuevo León	18.2	21.2	27.9	3.5	20.08
Jalisco	3.0	3.7	10.7	0.9	4.25
Tamaulipas	2.1	0.4	....	39.0	2.76
Hidalgo	2.2	3.0	....	1.0	2.18
Veracruz	0.3	1.3	2.0	8.1	1.30
Others	4.7	0.2	7.7	43.2	4.91
Total	100.0	100.0	100.0	100.0	100.00

Source: Cámara Nacional de la Industria del Hierro y del Acero, *Segundo Congreso Nacional de la Industria Siderúrgica*, p. 51.

are required.[47] When coal, ore, and scrap are considered, several tons of raw materials are used to produce one ton of finished steel. The iron ore used by AHMSA was originally from Durango and purchased from Fundidora, but is now from AHMSA's own mines, called La Perla, in Chihuahua.[48] AHMSA's coal was located in the Sabinas fields in Coahuila, near Monclova. The exact location in the city of Monclova hinged upon the availability of water from the Monclova River, huge quantities of water being essential to the production of iron and steel.

American Rolling Mills contracted with AHMSA to furnish technical help and advice for the construction and initial operation of the mill.[49] Parts of the blast furnace began to arrive in Monclova in April, 1942, but not until June, 1944, was it completed. The blast furnace, the open-hearth furnaces, and the rolling mill all went into full-scale operation in October, 1945, although records indicate some small amounts produced in 1944. The first production was the aforementioned steel plate used for construction of "Liberty Ships"

[47] Richard Hartshorne, "Location Factors in the Iron and Steel Industry," *Economic Geography* (July, 1928), pp. 241–243.
[48] Oscar Realme Rodríguez, "La Industria Siderúrgica Nacional," p. 110.
[49] Friedmann and Kalmanoff, *Joint International Business Ventures*, pp. 282–283.

in the United States at Port Arthur and New Orleans.[50] With the end of hostilities the steel plate was available for the domestic market. AHMSA was the first company to produce steel plate in Mexico and also the first to produce tin plate. Tin plate production requires a cold-rolling mill and new equipment was purchased; production of tin plate began in February, 1946.

The original blast furnace had a maximum daily output of 200 metric tons. Other equipment in the original operation included: two open-hearth furnaces, each of 65-ton capacity, one universal hot-rolling mill, two 4-high cold-reversing mills, and three centrifugal cast-iron-pipe mills. Also included were maintenance shops that were disproportionately large for the size of the plant. These large shops were necessary "in view of the non-availability of such shop services as is the case in most steel-producing centers in the United States."[51]

A breakdown of production by product is given in Table 4. By comparing data in Table 4 with that in Table 1 we note that in 1953 AHMSA's production of steel (measured in ingots) surpassed that of Fundidora. In that year AHMSA's production of steel ingots was 183,306 tons as compared to 137,002 tons for Fundidora. In the following year, 1954, AHMSA surpassed Fundidora in the production of pig iron, with a total of 137,114 tons, compared to 114,686 tons for Fundidora. AHMSA's yearly production of both steel and pig iron has exceeded that of Fundidora for every year since those years mentioned above.

In addition to Fundidora and AHMSA, there are two other integrated steel companies in Mexico: La Consolidada, S.A., and Hojalata y Lámina, S.A. La Consolidada is one of the older firms in Mexico. It was established as a private enterprise but was obtained by AHMSA in 1962 through an acquisition of 65 per cent of La Consolidada's capital stock.[52] La Consolidada has operations in four locations, one in Piedras Negras and the others in Lechería, Santa Clara, and Mexico City. The latter three, all in or near Mexico City, are rolling mills.

The operation in Piedras Negras is now integrated to the extent that a small blast furnace with a capacity of 220 tons per day supplies pig iron for the three Siemens-Martin open-hearth furnaces.

---

[50] Pape, "Five Years of Achievement," p. 58.
[51] *Ibid.*, pp. 58–59.
[52] Torón Villegas, *La Industria Siderúrgica Pesada*, p. 50.

TABLE 4

Production of Iron and Steel by
Altos Hornos de México, S.A. (1944–1960)
(Metric Tons)

Year	Pig Iron[1]	Steel Ingots[2]	Steel Plate[3]	Sheet Steel[3]	Tinplate[3]
1944	23,618	5,880	4,002	........[a]	....
1945	47,535	44,161	32,548	....	....
1946	72,733	63,731	38,219	9,787	2,373
1947	62,882	93,674	46,226	25,116	3,169
1948	59,915	96,618	41,131	25,163	5,112
1949	73,395	118,156	40,587	35,789	10,052
1950	108,451	123,442	36,425	43,565	11,785
1951	105,493	143,167	39,328	52,574	13,671
1952	118,692	166,750	50,869	55,224	13,015
1953	115,778	182,306	57,652	51,530	19,180
1954	137,114	219,174	63,620	69,197	24,334
1955	190,305[2]	256,075	72,897	75,231	24,517
1956[2]	205,789	314,172	....	....	....
1957[2]	203,121	355,636	....	....	....
1958[2]	256,038	353,534	....	....	....
1959[2]	316,310	415,467	....	....	....
1960[2]	443,770	550,000	....	....	....

Sources: [1] Cámara Nacional de la Industria del Hierro y del Acero, *Primero Congreso Nacional de la Industria Siderúrgica*, p. 87.
[2] Carlos A. Rivera Rangel, "La Siderúrgica y la Integración Industrial de México," pp. 29–31.
[3] Cámara Nacional de la Industria del Hierro y del Acero, *Segundo Congreso Nacional de la Industria Siderúrgica*, p. 52.
[a] Data not available.

Two of these steel-making furnaces have a capacity of 80 tons each and the third a capacity of 60 tons. Prior to the erection of the blast furnace the Siemens-Martin furnaces were charged with scrap imported from the United States or pig iron purchased from Fundidora in Monterrey.[53]

The rolling mills in the Federal District use steel ingots produced in Piedras Negras.[54] These mills produce various shapes and rods for construction in addition to wire, cable, springs, nuts, bolts, and

[53] Realme Rodríguez, "La Industria Siderúrgica Nacional," p. 111.
[54] Torón Villegas, *La Industria Siderúrgica Pesada*, p. 54.

TABLE 5

Production of Steel by La Consolidada (1944–1960)
(Tons of Steel Ingots)

Year	Production	Year	Production
1944	33,467	1953	88,692
1945	29,446	1954	81,403
1946	31,520	1955	94,145
1947	44,221	1956	105,131
1948	48,940	1957	119,493
1949	65,370	1958	151,051
1950	69,624	1959	161,797
1951	84,209	1960	160,000
1952	94,012		

Source: Carlos A. Rivera Rangel, "La Siderúrgica y la Integración Industrial de México, p. 31.

screws. Table 5 gives steel production, in terms of ingots, for La Consolidada.

The third largest company is Hojalata y Lámina, S.A. (commonly referred to by its initials: HYLSA), which is the newest of the large companies. Like Fundidora, it is located in Monterrey, Mexico's industrial center. HYLSA was established in 1946. The investment was made entirely from privately held funds. HYLSA, together with its affiliate Fierro Esponja, S.A., forms an integrated operation for making iron and steel. As first constituted in 1946, HYLSA did not have an integrated operation. Scrap was reduced in electric furnaces and rolled into flat products, making it only an industry of transformation. The operation proved successful, but when expansion was considered, the need for raw materials (scrap) proved to be a major problem. A scarcity of domestic scrap and violently fluctuating world prices resulted in efforts to find a way to obtain pig iron for the steel furnaces. The classic methods were considered but investment in a modern blast furnace was considered to be beyond the ability or desires of the company. In addition, the level of efficient operation for a blast furnace (1,000 tons per day) was beyond the projected level of utilization.[55] Consequently another approach to the problem was taken which resulted in the

[55] *Ibid.*, pp. 95–96.

establishment of a pilot plant, with a daily capacity of 50 tons, for the production of sponge iron.[56] Sponge iron is a porous iron obtained by direct reduction of the ore. The direct method of reduction harks back to the previously discussed Catalan forge of fifteenth- and sixteenth-century vintage.[57] Although the reduction process was similar, there were, of course, major differences. The Catalan forge reduced the ore through direct contact of the ore with coal while the sponge-iron process of HYLSA uses natural gas.

The pilot plant was a success, and by the end of 1957 Fierro Esponja had established a plant with a daily capacity of 200 tons of sponge iron. This capacity was later increased to 250 tons. As the demand for steel grew, plans for expansion were made, and in 1960

TABLE 6

Production of Steel and Sponge Iron
by Hojalata y Lámina, S.A. (1944–1960)
(Tons)

Year	Steel Ingots	Sponge Iron
1944	5,800	....
1945	11,650	....
1946	15,600	....
1947	13,450	....
1948	21,000	....
1949	21,300	....
1950	34,750	....
1951	41,754	....
1952	42,961	....
1953	44,561	....
1954	66,876	....
1955	96,526	....
1956	118,895	....
1957	156,288	....
1958	149,170	....
1959	254,685	72,000
1960	250,000	108,000

Source: Carlos A. Rivera Rangel, "La Siderúrgica y la Integración Industrial de México, pp. 29–31.

[56] *Ibid.*, p. 97.
[57] *Ibid.*, p. 96.

a second plant with a capacity of 500 tons daily was put into operation, giving the company a total sponge-iron capacity of 750 tons per day. This sponge iron is reduced in the electric steel-making furnaces of the parent company and rolled by them into an ever increasing variety of flat-rolled products. Table 6 shows the production of steel (ingots) and sponge iron by HYLSA and its subsidiary.

In 1955, Tubos de Acero de México, S.A. (commonly referred to as TAMSA), began production. Located in Veracruz, it is Mexico's largest mill devoted exclusively to pipe. Originally the pipe was fabricated from semifinished steel which was purchased from other firms. However, in 1959 TAMSA began production of its own steel by reducing imported scrap in electric furnaces.[58] Original investments had totalled 120,260,000 pesos; by 1963 this had been supplemented to a sum of 571,340,000 pesos.[59] Table 7 details the production of TAMSA.

The company was promoted by a group of private Mexican investors who enlisted some financial support from foreign investors, principally in Italy but also in Sweden and France.[60] Twenty per

TABLE 7

Production of Steel Ingots and Pipe by TAMSA (1954–1963)
(Metric Tons)

Year	Steel Ingots	Pipe
1954	--------	5,352[a]
1955	--------	35,886
1956	--------	49,664
1957	--------	73,058
1958	42,460	98,570
1959	100,000	108,872
1960	160,670	123,180
1961	161,270	109,040
1962	161,920	120,150
1963	195,740	127,140

Source: Tubos de Acero de México, *Informe Anual de 1963*.
[a] Experimental production.

[58] Tubos de Acero de México, *Informe Anual de 1963*, p. 33.
[59] *Ibid.*, p. 31.
[60] Friedmann and Kalmanoff, *Joint International Business Ventures*, pp. 369–370.

cent of the original investment was subscribed by Nacional Financiera.

TAMSA is now the principal source of pipe for Mexico's petroleum industry (Petroleos Mexicanos). Previously all seamless pipe requirements had been furnished by imports.

Although the larger firms account for most of the output, the Latin American Institute of Iron and Steel listed fifty-three firms making iron and steel products in Mexico during 1962.[61] The more important of these firms are listed in Table 8.

Total steel-making capacity (ingots) in 1961 was 2,290,000 tons per year, which breaks down as follows:[62]

AHMSA	690,000 tons per year
Fundidora	600,000 tons per year
HYLSA	300,000 tons per year
La Consolidada	180,000 tons per year
Nonintegrated firms	520,000 tons per year

Of the total, 1,470,000 tons of capacity was accounted for by the seventeen Siemens-Martin furnaces in operation in Mexico. Distribution of these furnaces was: seven each to AHMSA and Fundidora and three to La Consolidada in Piedras Negras. The 820,000 tons of capacity accounted for by HYLSA and the nonintegrated firms represented thirty-six electric furnaces, six of which were owned by HYLSA.

The steel-making capacity was complemented by a pig-iron capacity of 955,000 tons and a sponge-iron capacity totaling 245,000 tons per year. This capacity was broken down as follows:[63]

AHMSA	560,000 tons per year
Fundidora	315,000 tons per year
La Consolidada	80,000 tons per year
Fierro Esponja	245,000 tons per year

The pig-iron capacity consisted of two blast furnaces each at AHMSA and Fundidora and one at La Consolidada in Piedras Negras. The 245,000 tons of sponge-iron capacity was provided by the two installations for the reduction of iron ore with natural gas located with HYLSA's affiliate in Monterrey, Fierro Esponja.

[61] Instituto Latinoamericano del Fierro y el Acero, *Reportorio de las Empresas Siderúrgicas*, pp. 175–209.

[62] Comité para Programación de la Industria Siderúrgica, *Programación del Desarrollo de la Industria Siderúrgica Mexicana*, Table 3.

[63] *Ibid.*

TABLE 8

Iron and Steel Plants in Mexico (1962)

Company	City	State
1. Acero Solar, S.A.	Querétaro	Querétaro
2. Aceros Coras, S.A.	San Juan Ixhuatepec	México
3. Aceros de México, S.A.	El Mezquital	Nuevo León
4. Aceros de Sonora, S.A.	Guaymas	Sonora
5. Aceros Ecatepec, S.A.	Tulpetlac	México
6. Aceros Laminados, S.A.	Tlalnepantla	México
7. Aceros Nacionales, S.A.	Tlalnepantla	México
8. Altos Hornos de México, S.A.	Monclova	Coahuila
9. Barras y Perfiles, S.A.	Atzcapotzalco	D.F.
10. Central Laminadora, S.A.	México	D.F.
11. Compañía Fundirora de Chihuahua, S.A.	Chihuahua	Chihuahua
12. Compañía Fundidora de Fierro y Acero de Monterrey, S.A.	Monterrey	Nuevo León
13. Fundiciones de Hierro y Acero, S.A.	México	D.F.
14. Fundirora de Aceros Tepeyac, S.A.	Santa Clara	México
15. Fundidora y Laminadora Anáhuac, S.A.	México	D.F.
16. Herramientas México. S.A.	Tlalnepantla	México
17. Hojalata y Lámina, S.A.	Monterrey	Nuevo León
18. Industrias Monterrey, S.A.	Monterrey	Nuevo León
19. Kreimerman, S.A.	Santa Clara	México
20. La Consolidada, S.A.	Piedras Negras	Coahuila
	Lechería	México
	México	D.F.
21. Laminadora Atzcapotzalco, S.A.	Atzcapotzalco	D.F.
22. Laminadora Barniedo, S.A.	México	D.F.
23. Laminadoras Unidas, S.A.	México	D.F.
24. Pizarrones de México	San Bartolo Nancalpan	México
25. Siderúrgica Mexicana, S.A.	México	D.F.
26. Siderúrgica Potosina, S.A. de C.V.	San Luis Potosí	S.L.P.
27. Tubos de Acero de México, S.A.	Veracruz	Veracruz

Sources: Cámara Nacional de la Industria del Hierro y del Acero, *Comercio Exterior* (English edition).

As will be detailed in later chapters, Mexico has abundant supplies of fuels and raw materials for supplying an iron and steel industry. As early as the beginning of this century specific economic conditions warranted the establishment of a steel industry. These conditions were centered around the growth of the railroad and petroleum industries. It was not until World War II that general economic conditions seemed propitious for the establishment of a flat-rolled products sector to the industry. As will be shown, the growth of the industry has been phenomenal since the mid-forties.

2. Government Promotion, Participation, and Regulation

Prior to the 1940's the main interest of the Mexican government toward steel was reflected through the normal channels of control of international trade, such as tariffs on imports, import licensing, and the rationing of foreign exchange to importers. While there was an aspect of protection involved in pre-1941 tariffs, for the most part they served as a source of revenue. A large proportion of the volume of steel imports was represented by flat-rolled products, none of which were produced in Mexico, so that in such cases no measure of protection to existing industry was involved. Rafael Izquierdo tells us, "Protectionism in modern Mexico begins in earnest with the second World War."[1] The second World War brought with it shortages of those manufactured goods that Mexico had imported to satisfy its internal demand. With these shortages, "both the government and private industry became keenly aware of the advantages to be gained . . . by restricting imports of goods that could be produced locally and at the same time facilitating imports of capital goods."[2] It was at this time that the Mexican government became active in the promotion and regulation of the steel industry, in addition to undertaking to protect it from imports.

Although there was present in Mexico a steel industry at the beginning of the decade of the 1940's, it was small and produced a relatively small number of products. In 1940 only 149,414 tons of steel were produced in Mexico, and of these there were no flat-rolled products. During that year steel consumption totaled 276,144 tons, of which 126,730 tons, or 46 per cent, were imported. The produc-

[1] Rafael Izquierdo, "Protectionism in Mexico," in Raymond Vernon (ed.), *Public Policy and Private Enterprise in Mexico*, p. 243.
[2] *Ibid.*

tion of flat-rolled products requires mills that can be operated efficiently only at high levels of production, and while consumption of these products was at a significant level, it was nowhere near the level necessary to allow the economies of scale that would be required if the new industry in Mexico was to compete with imports. (For an appraisal of economies of scale in the Mexican steel industry, see Chapter 4.)

For the years 1937 through 1941, the average import of flat-rolled products was 40,500 tons, broken down as follows: [3]

Steel plate	7,000 tons
Sheet steel	16,500 tons
Tinplate	17,000 tons

According to Pape this level of imports was considered "sufficient— to support a small, specialized, well-founded plant."[4] It was originally planned to establish such a mill, using imported steel strip as the raw material. The would-be promoters were prominent members of the private sector. In the end it was neither technical difficulties nor considerations of cost that led to the scrapping of plans for a rolling mill using imported raw materials. It was fear of dominance by foreign suppliers.

Preliminary studies indicated that a mill based on rerolling imported steel would be entirely at the mercy of foreign suppliers, a situation which was not likely to be in the interests of the proposed new enterprise or in the national interests of Mexico.[5]

Placing this attitude in its historical context, it does not seem unlikely that fear of foreign control of supply would be prominent in the decision-making process. The era of Cárdenas had just closed, negotiations were yet in progress regarding oil expropriations by the Mexican government, and discontent with foreign electrical companies was also prevalent.

The alternative to using imported steel strip as a raw material was the use of domestic raw materials, particularly iron ore and coal. (Discussion of the Mexican government's role in the establishment of AHMSA entails repetition of some small parts of Chapter I.) The adoption of this alternative would have required a much greater investment in capital equipment because the proposed plant

---

[3] H. R. Pape, "Five Years of Achievement at Altos Hornos Steel Company," *Basic Industries in Texas and Northern Mexico.*
[4] *Ibid.*
[5] *Ibid.*

would have been required to perform all of the basic operations of an integrated mill. Although members of the private sector had initiated the plans, this group was unable to mobilize the financial resources sufficient to make the investment.[6] Besides, the private sector was at that same time expending funds to implement plans to expand steel production by Fundidora in Monterrey. In 1942, that company began construction of a second blast furnace and expansion of its steel-making department.[7]

At this point the Mexican government decided to step into the picture and play a major entrepreneurial role in the development of the domestic steel industry. It was decided that the new steel firm should be an integrated operation, employing domestic raw materials; the Nacional Financiera, S.A., was assigned the task of handling the government's part of this venture. The Nacional Financiera is the Mexican government's entrepreneurial arm. Use of the word "entrepreneurial" is designed to convey the idea that it is more than just a financing institution. In addition to aiding in the financing of AHMSA, it acted as a promoter, and after establishment of the firm it acted in an ownership capacity as the principal stockholder. This is described by Blair:

Private financial resources proved inadequate for an enterprise of the size and scope of Altos Hornos. NAFIN [the commonly used abbreviation for Nacional Financiera, S.A.,] stepped in, borrowed 6 million dollars from the Export-Import Bank of Washington, subscribed to securities and extended credits to finance the new firm. . . . At the end of 1945, NAFIN held all of the bonds, more than three fourths of the preferred stock, and over one fourth of the common stock of the firm—security investments totaling 61.5 million pesos. Two years later, NAFIN became majority stockholder and began to make of Altos Hornos a showcase of public intervention in the industrial sphere.[8]

The plans actively under way for AHMSA called for an average annual production as follows:
Tinplate ....18,000 tons
Cold-rolled sheets ....15,000 tons

---

[6] Calvin P. Blair, "Nacional Financiera, Entrepreneurship in a Mixed Economy," in Raymond Vernon (ed.), *Public Policy and Private Enterprise in Mexico*, p. 213.

[7] Carlos Prieto, "La Industria Siderúrgica," *México, 50 Años de Revolución*, I: *La Economía*, 217.

[8] Blair, "Nacional Financiera," pp. 215–216.

Steel plate ....15,000 tons
Cast-iron pipe .... 7,000 tons[9]

With an integrated steel mill producing at a level of 55,000 tons annually, internal economies of scale would not be enjoyed. In addition, many of the external economies of scale that are enjoyed in highly industrialized countries were not available to the new company. Among these external economies that are present in the United States are: highly developed sources of power, a wealth of skilled workers and technically trained personnel, well-explored raw-material reserves that are efficiently mined, and a well-developed network of transportation. By virtue of the small scale of the steel companies and the underdeveloped nature of the economy in general, prices for Mexican steel were higher than the prices of steel imports (see Appendix A). One writer points out that while the entire industry was inefficient, AHMSA, being greatly over-capitalized for its level of production, had the highest per-unit cost. Other firms producing the same products looked to AHMSA as a price leader and raised their prices accordingly.[10] This would seem to be an interesting case of a government firm acting as price leader in an oligopoly situation in which some might contend the public was done a disservice.

Regardless of the system used to arrive at market prices, the industry as a whole was inefficient and needed protection against imports. Although some semblance of a steel industry was present in 1940, it would seem acceptable to study the protection policy in the context of the "infant industry" argument. Put succinctly, this argument states that new industry must be protected from imports until it has had time to become efficient enough to be able to compete with those imports. Within this context we shall check to see if the protected industry has grown and if it has become more efficient vis-à-vis those industries that would provide the imports in the absence of the domestic industry.

In addition to protection of domestic industry, a concomitant motive for protection was the stated policy of import substitution. Reasons for wanting to substitute a domestic manufacture for an imported one can include: (1) the desire to increase the degree of

[9] Pape, "Five Years of Achievement," p. 52.
[10] Oscar Realme Rodríguez, "La Industria Siderúrgica Nacional," p. 108. The source refers specifically to the firms Hojalata y Lámina, S.A., and Campos Hermanos, both of which were, in 1946, nonintegrated operations rolling steel from (usually imported) semifinished steel.

economic independence, especially in the face of deteriorating terms of trade for primary products; (2) the desire to save foreign exchange for other types of goods, especially capital goods; (3) the employment provided by the domestic industry; and (4) national pride. Although an import-substitution policy complements a policy of infant-industry protection, it is not necessary that every policy of infant-industry protection also be an effective import-substitution policy. A protective policy might possibly call for tariff barriers to be only so high as to make a domestic product competitive with its foreign counterpart, but not high enough to exclude imports on basis of price.

The Mexican government uses, chiefly, two types of controls on imports: the general instrument of the tariff and the quantitative instrument of import licensing. The tariff applies equally to all who import the item in question and therefore it places no direct control on the level of imports. On the other hand, quantitative controls are applied selectively. The Secretaría de Hacienda (finance minister) is responsible for the administration of tariff policy and the Secretaría de Industria y Comercio (secretary of industry and commerce) has similar responsibility for quantitative controls.[11]

Quantitative controls are administered through an import-licensing system. Import licenses are required for about three fourths of the items imported into Mexico. For certain of these products . . . there are annual quotas, which are allocated to importers in proportion to the amounts they previously imported. For other products, having no quotas, licenses are granted in accordance with the circumstances, and the government has great latitude in regulating the volume of imports.[12]

Tariffs as applied to steel consist of two parts, first, a specific rate per physical unit (pesos per kilogram) and second, an ad valorem rate. Table 9 lists tariffs in force between 1939 and 1963 for several important steel products. Also shown are the dates when quantitative controls were applied to each particular product and the date, if any, for the withdrawal of quantitative controls. No specific information as to the size of quotas is presented. Further, import licenses are granted on an individual basis with each case judged on its merits and, here again, no specific information was available to this writer.

[11] Izquierdo, "Protectionism in Mexico," p. 252.
[12] *Ibid.*, pp. 254–255.

TABLE 9

History of Tariffs on Steel Products (1935–1961)

Product and Tariff Code	Effective Date of Tariff		Specific (Pesos per kilo)	Ad Valorem (%)
Tinplate	Feb.	15, 1944	$ 0.20	....
(670.06.01)	Sept.	16, 1945	(Import only with permission of Sría. de Hacienda y Crédito Público)	
	Dec.	13, 1947	0.15	30
	Oct.	22, 1948	0.10	25
	April	14, 1958	0.10	30
Pipe	Nov.	13, 1947	0.01	10
(nongalvanized)	Sept.	30, 1948	0.10	30
(670.03.98)	Jan.	4, 1951	0.50	10
	Jan.	19, 1951	(Import only with permission of Sría. de Hacienda y Crédito Público)	
	July	25, 1953	0.60	10
	Nov.	25, 1954	0.90	10
	April	14, 1958	0.90	12
	March	23, 1961	1.50	25
Sheet Steel	April	30, 1938	2.50	....
(more than 15 cm in width)	June	15, 1942	(Import only with permission of Sría. de Economía Nacional)	
(670.05.00)				
	Dec.	13, 1947	0.05	30
	Feb.	19, 1948	0.10	35
	Oct.	27, 1948	0.10	25
	Jan.	19, 1951	0.30	10
	Sept.	28, 1954	0.52	1
	April	24, 1958	0.55	2
Iron and Steel Rods	Jan.	8, 1937	0.15	....
(670.01.99)	Nov.	16, 1945	(Import only with permission of Sría. de Hacienda y Crédito Público)	
	Dec.	13, 1947	0.01 (100 kilos)	5
	Feb.	19, 1948	0.01 (100 kilos)	1
	July	29, 1953	0.40	10
	Nov.	25, 1954	0.50	15

TABLE 9—(*Continued*)

Product and Tariff Code	Effective Date of Tariff		Specific (Pesos per kilo)	Ad Valorem (%)
	April	24, 1958	0.50	20
	April	13, 1961	0.55	25
Railway Material (axles and rails) (273.00.01)	April	4, 1935	$ 0.30	....
	June	15, 1942	(Import only with permission of Sría. de Economía Nacional)	
	Jan.	19, 1951	0.05	3
	Nov.	25, 1954	0.07	3
	April	24, 1958	0.07	5
Steel Plate (nonspecified) (670.05.99)	April	30, 1938	0.03	....
	Nov.	13, 1947	0.10	30
	Sept.	30, 1948	(Import only with permission of Sría. de Economía Nacional)	
	Oct.	27, 1948	0.10	25
	Jan.	4, 1951	0.30	10
	Sept.	28, 1954	0.46	1
	April	24, 1958	0.50	2
	April	3, 1961	1.50	10
Steel Wire (670.02.01)	Feb.	26, 1937	0.14	....
	June	15, 1942	(Import only with permission of Sría. de Economía Nacional)	
	Dec.	12, 1947	0.05	30
	Oct.	27, 1948	0.05	25
	Jan.	19, 1951	(Import only with permission of Sría. de Hacienda y Crédito Público)	
	Feb.	14, 1954	0.10	30
	April	24, 1958	0.10	35

Source: Direct investigation of the records of the Departamento de Estudios Hacendarios of the Secretaría de Hacienda y Crédito Público, August, 1964.

It will be noted that although tariffs on steel products date back to the 1930's, it was not until 1947 that the additional ad valorem duty was added. It will also be noted from Table 9 that the year 1947 marked a general rise in the level of tariff protection.

FIGURE 1

Replacement of Steel Plate Imports

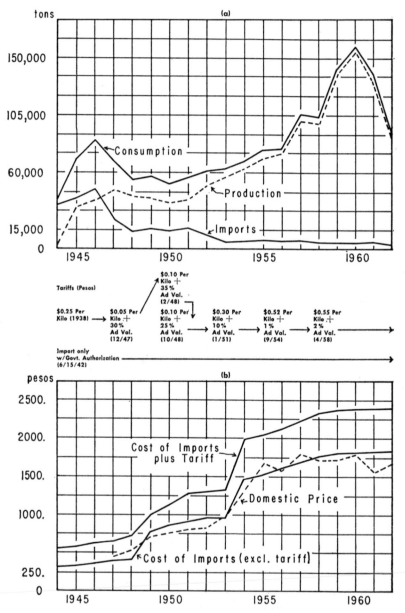

The effect of the protection policy as a tool of import substitution will be evaluated by studying the history of flat-rolled products for the period 1944–1962. Flat-rolled products were selected for study because that was the area of production in which the new firms (AHMSA and, in 1946, HYLSA) concentrated their efforts. Then there will follow an evaluation of the policy of infant-industry protection which will use the same data.

In Figures 1, 2, and 3, "cost of imports" is defined as the per-ton price quoted in the United States plus transportation costs from the mills to Mexico. "Cost of imports plus tariff" includes both specific and ad valorem tariffs in addition to United States price plus transportation. Sources and derivations of the data used may be found in Appendix A.

The first flat-rolled product to be produced in significant quantities in Mexico was steel plate, whose production was begun by AHMSA in 1944. All the demand prior to that year had been satisfied by imports. Some small quantities of sheet steel were produced as early as 1941. As shown in Figure 1 while consumption grew throughout the period studied (1944–1960), production grew at a higher rate, resulting in the diminution of the level of imports to the point that by the period 1960–1962, imports accounted for but a very small percentage of total consumption of steel plate. Figure 1(b) indicates that for eight of the nineteen years of domestic production, the price of domestic steel plate was higher than the cost of importing steel plate. The import cost includes an allowance for transportation costs from the producing center to a Mexican port. And it is especially significant that this was the case in the early years of steel plate production, 1944–1948, from the point of view of the infant-industry argument. By virtue of the tariff wall, the cost of imports plus tariff was higher in every year than the cost of the domestic product. Therefore, as domestic production was increased so as to approach the level of consumption, the substitution of domestic steel plate for imports of that product was nearly complete.

This apparent success in replacing imports is observed in Figure 2 (tin plate) and Figure 3 (sheet steel). Whereas the physical level of imports declined over the period for both steel plate and tin plate, the level of imports of sheet steel remained fairly constant. Nevertheless, the import-substitution policy can be called a success with very little qualification since the level of consumption of sheet steel

FIGURE 2

Replacement of Tinplate Imports

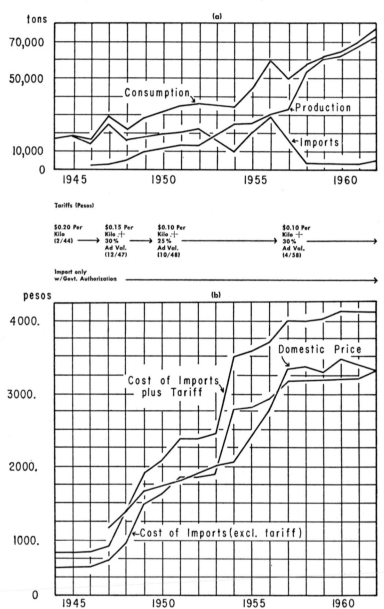

FIGURE 3

Replacement of Sheet Steel Imports

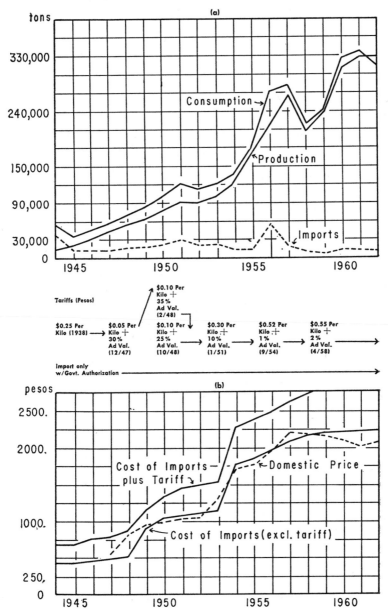

increased greatly and by 1962 production exceeded consumption. Also, as in the case of steel plate, the prices of sheet and tin plate were often higher than import cost. In each case the domestic price was the higher in the early years of production. The tin plate price has remained generally above import costs, except for the period 1954–1956. An interesting phenomenon is observed for prices of all three products for the year 1954. In that year Mexico devalued the peso from an exchange ratio of 11.561 U.S. cents per peso to 8.00 U.S. cents per peso. This action would be expected automatically to raise the peso price of steel imports, which in fact happened as can be observed in the (b) sections of Figures 1, 2, and 3. In each case the cost of imports rose more than the price of the domestic product; nevertheless, the domestic price quickly caught up with and surpassed the import cost. In the case of steel plate, the domestic price dropped behind import cost for only one year, whereas the domestic price of sheet and tin plate remained lower than import costs for three years. Following devaluation, one force that would be expected to exert an upward push on domestic prices is the cost of imported factors of production which include raw materials (especially scrap) and capital equipment. As shown in Chapter 3 the percentage of unit cost of steel going as payment to foreign factors is significant. This of course means that when the peso was devalued, rates of payments to foreign factors increased in terms of pesos. Judging from this small sample, one might speculate that devaluation is of only very short-run value as a means of increasing import costs of steel relative to domestic price.

In practically every year it appears that the tariff wall was sufficiently high to place the cost of imports above domestic costs for all three steel products. Government policy was successful in replacing imports, but the efficacy of the tariff wall in terms of the traditional infant-industry argument must also be evaluated. Obviously the new industry (the flat-rolled portion of the steel industry) became firmly established. Both AHMSA and HYLSA appear to be on firm foundation and both are presently implementing expansion plans. But the establishment of the industry is only one aspect of the infant-industry argument. As the new industry substitutes its product for imports, it should grow in efficiency as measured in terms of price. Since steel prices are dynamic, the prices of domestic steel for 1962 cannot be measured against 1947 domestic prices to see if the industry has become more efficient. However, the efficiency of the domestic industry can be measured against the efficiency of the established industry in the United States. By this criterion, the domestic industry appears to have become more efficient vis-à-vis the world steel industry. This result is most apparent with plate and sheet, where for the five-year period 1958–1962 the domestic price was lower than the cost of imports. In the case of tin plate the domestic price fell below the import cost for only three years, 1954–1956, apparently as the result of the peso devaluation of 1954. Nevertheless the domestic price as a percentage of import cost has declined.

To sum up, tariff protection and quantitative controls applied to steel plate, sheet steel, and tin plate were successful in effecting a substitution of domestically produced steel for foreign imports and in promoting the growth of the domestic steel industry. This growth is witnessed by the steady growth of domestic steel production.

In addition to direct application of tariff controls and import licensing to steel products, such tools have given an indirect boost to the steel industry when applied to finished products with significant steel content. Of particular importance has been governmental promotion of domestic auto manufacture through the granting of concessions and stringent import bans. These bans apply to many of the major parts as well as to the assembled auto. This policy has induced a number of foreign auto makers to invest in plants and equipment in Mexico. Where the auto industry consumed 20,467 tons of steel in 1962, it has been projected that this figure will rise to 115,500 tons by 1970. Whereas government policy as applied to the auto industry has inducement effects on the steel industry, it is the government-promoted AHMSA that will supply much of the inputs of the auto industry, especially of sheet steel. Without a domestic steel supply, it would be much less feasible to substitute domestically manufactured autos for imported ones.

The extent of direct government participation in the economy is illustrated by the fact that Fundidora is the largest privately owned firm in Mexico in terms of capitalization, but ranks no higher than eleventh among all firms, behind ten publicly owned companies.[13]

Tax exemptions have also played a role in the building of Mexico's steel industry. On December 30, 1936, certain tax exemptions to promote domestic industry were decreed and among the industries covered were iron and steel. This principle was carried

[13] *Mexico City News*, June 30, 1964, p. 21–A.

forward in several pieces of legislation. The *Ley de Industrias de Transformación* of 1941, the *Ley de Fomento de Industrias de Transformación* of 1946, and finally, the *Ley de Fomento de Industrias Nuevas y Necesarias* of 1946 all carried the principle of granting tax subsidies to industries deemed necessary for implementing the government's policies of import substitution and industrialization.[14] The principle is expressed in the wording of the 1955 law:

Son industrias necesarias, las que tengan por objeto la manufactura o fabricación de mercancias que se produzcan en el pais en cantidad insuficiente para satisfacer las necesidades del consumo nacional, siempre que el deficit sea considerable y no provenga de causas transitorias.[15]

The first exemptions granted to the steel industry were decreed in 1940 and included sheet and plate, neither of which were in production at the time.[16] One of the first and largest concessions went to AHMSA in 1944, for a duration of five years, later extended to ten years. Exemptions were of three classes: (1) relaxation of tariffs on imports of capital goods, (2) exemption from income tax, and (3) exemption from business taxes. For the period 1949–1955 the tax concessions to the steel industry amounted to 252,041,000 pesos.[17] Of this total, 85,782,000 pesos were conceded on imports of capital goods, 102,949,000 on income, and 63,310,000 on business income.

Government influence, however, does not stop with import restrictions and tax concessions. The government exerts influence upon the domestic marketing practices of the steel industry. This control is accomplished in two ways: directly, through the implementation of law, and indirectly, through the route of exercising oligopoly power through AHMSA, which is now the largest company in the industry. The direct control is through the implementation of Article 28 of the Mexican Constitution through the public law, *Ley sobre Atribuciones del Ejecutivo en Materia Económica* of December 30, 1950. This law empowers the Secretaría de In-

[14] Carlos A. Rivera Rangel, "La Siderúrgica y la Integración Industrial de México," p. 68.

[15] *Ibid.*, pp. 68–69.

[16] *Ibid.*, p. 70.

[17] *Ibid.*, p. 72.

dustria y Comercio to set maximum prices on certain products, among which are steel products.

But the government's power in control of prices and markets is more pervasive than the mere legal aspects. The government is involved as owner of the largest firm in the industry and the public sector is a large factor in the consumption of steel, its many-faceted operations providing market outlets for all types of steel. Table 10 gives a dramatic presentation of the government's impact as purchaser.

In Table 10, "government sector" refers to the Mexican government and decentralized agencies, and "private sector" includes the transforming, construction, and mining industries.[18] It is obvious that the government could wield great power by use of contracts and purchase orders. With AHMSA presently the largest steel producer and with government a major consumer, public officials, by favoring the government's own company, could slap the wrists

TABLE 10

Breakdown of Steel Consumption by Government
and Private Sectors
(Percentage of Total Consumption)

Product	Government Sector	Private Sector
Rails and Maintenance of Way	98.0	2.0
Railway Wheels and Axles	97.5	2.5
Structural Shapes	24.5	75.5
Plate	45.0	55.0
Sheet	4.0	96.0
Tinplate	1.0	99.0
Cast-Iron Pipe	95.0	5.0
Welded Pipe	60.0	40.0
Seamless Pipe	90.0	10.0
Wire, Bar, and Merchant Sections	40.0	60.0
Mining Material	2.0	98.0
Casting, etc.	30.0	70.0

Source: United Nations, *A Study of the Iron and Steel Industry in Latin America*, II, 441.

[18] United Nations, *A Study of the Iron and Steel Industry in Latin America*, II, 441.

of private firms. Here, it may be said that while there is little or no evidence of government pressure on the private firms, the fact that pressure could quickly be brought to bear undoubtedly acts as a factor of control in itself.

In fact, there is strong evidence at hand to show that the Mexican government has on occasion taken steps to protect the interests of the private sector of the steel industry from AHMSA when the latter attempted an apparent power play. For example, AHMSA supplied the raw material (sheet steel) to a private pipe manufacturer in Monterrey, Tubacero (Tubos de Acero de Monterrey, S.A.). AHMSA reputedly brought pressure to bear (by virtue of being the raw material supplier) to have majority ownership sold to it. This move was probably prompted by a proposed major pipe line by PEMEX, for which AHMSA had visions of supplying the pipe. According to Blair, the private sector then brought political pressure to bear directly through the office of the President of the Republic, forcing AHMSA to relax its own pressures and settle for a minority share of the stock.[19]

NAFIN has not limited its financial assistance to the public sector. During the period 1942–1963, NAFIN served as intermediary in obtaining foreign loans totaling $72,411,000 for various firms in the industry.[20] This figure does not include loans involving the coal industry. A breakdown of the major portion of these loans is given in Table 11. NAFIN was instrumental in the financing of such steel-using firms as Constructora Nacional de Carros de Ferrocarril, S.A., and Siderúrgica Nacional, S.A.

As regards competition for markets among the various firms, the situation seems to be similar to the oligopolistic behavior of steel firms in the United States. Blair says:

> In fact, the principal steel companies, both public and private, operate under a system of "accords" and of official prices fixed so that vested interests will not be prejudiced by too much competition. If the private sector is at all handicapped, it is certainly not helpless.[21]

A rationalization of collusion was eloquently phrased in a public statement by an industry official addressing the National Chamber of Iron and Steel Industry:

[19] Blair, "Nacional Financiera," p. 234.
[20] Nacional Financiera, *Informe Anual, 1964*, p. 134.
[21] Blair, "Nacional Financiera," p. 234.

TABLE 11

Foreign Loans to Iron and Steel Firms in Which
NAFIN Served as Intermediary (1942–1963)
(Thousands of U.S. Dollars)

Firm	Financial Institution	Total Loans (1942–1963)
Altos Hornos de México, S.A.	Export-Import Bank	45,900
	Chase Manhattan Bank	5,000
	Others	9,066
Hojalata y Lámina, S.A.	Export-Import Bank	3,600
La Consolidada, S.A.	Export-Import Bank	1,500
	Others	129
Tubos de Acero de México, S.A.	Others	4,885

Source: Nacional Financiera, S.A., *Informe Anual, 1964*, p. 134.

Debemos reconocer que la competencia, de hecho, es un verdadero estímulo para el acercamiento y progreso de la economía y del bienestar. . . . Hay, pues, competencias leales, hechas a la luz del día por medios justos y competencias desleales, hechas por medios injustos. . . .

Porque el precio normal y justo no es más que uno y así como en circunstancias ordinarios no es lícito aprovecharse de empresas en mal estado financiero para comprar sus productos por debajo del costo, así tampoco se puede poner un precio notablemente inferior al normal y justo, aunque se trate directamente de conseguir un monopolio que sólo puede venir por la ruina de un tercero.

Vivir y dejar vivir, es el principio que debe guiar al gerente en sus relaciones con los competidores. (Emphasis added)[22]

By virtue of producing different types of steel products, AHMSA and Fundidora, Mexico's two largest steel mills, do not have grounds for competition for much of the production of each.

To the economist trained in the United States, with his anti-trust background, it may at first seem ludicrous that a firm owned by the government would actively join in collusion with private firms to "fix" prices and share markets. Yet when it is realized that the overall goal of the government is the achievement of economic development, to which steel is a major contributor, the policy of

[22] Andrés Latapi, "Concepto y Responsibilidades de la Gerencia," in Cámara Nacional de la Industria del Hierro y del Acero, *Tercer Congreso Nacional de la Industria Siderúrgica*, pp. 114–115.

live-and-let-live has a more rational context. Some day in the future, when public officials are satisfied with the level of steel production, some competitive pressure could conceivably be brought to bear on the less efficient firms.

The conclusion is inescapable that the Mexican government, by virtue of wearing the three separate hats of purchaser, regulator, and owner, has played a significant role in the recent history of the iron and steel industry and will undoubtedly continue to play a unique role in the future.

There is little doubt that the tariff barrier erected against foreign steel was a major factor in the growth of the Mexican steel industry. Without some method of lowering domestic prices relative to import cost, domestically produced flat-rolled products could not have competed for the Mexican market. The tariff was chosen as a major tool for altering the cost of imports relative to domestic prices. To say that the tariff and import licensing controls were relatively successful in replacing imports with domestic steel does not mean that these policy tools were the only ones available with which to implement an import replacement policy nor does it mean that they are the best tools. The domestic price could be lowered both absolutely and in relation to imports by use of a production subsidy which, by virtue of lowering price, might lead to greater steel consumption. This possibility is discussed in Chapter 4.

3. Foreign Exchange Costs and Import Substitution

This chapter is designed to give additional insight into the nature and extent of foreign exchange savings derived from the substitution of domestic steel for imported steel. Here the concern is with the determination of the amount of foreign exchange saved per unit of domestic output substituted for a comparable import. The level of foreign exchange savings would involve the additional determination of the number of units involved in replacement as well as general equilibrium considerations such as the effect of increased national income (from investment in steel) upon the level of imports. Such general considerations are beyond the scope of this chapter.

The thesis is that the planner must go behind the unit cost of steel and analyze the origins and costs of the various inputs of the domestic steel industry to determine the amount of foreign exchange per unit of product to be saved by a policy of import substitution. A simple comparison of domestic versus foreign costs on a per unit basis will likely prove very deceptive and lead to an overestimation of the amount of foreign exchange to be saved by virtue of the substitution. In Chapter 4 it will be contended that the level of output is also a determinant of the amount of foreign exchange savings per unit of product through economies of scale.

The typical underdeveloped country is hard put for foreign exchange with which to purchase goods from the industrialized countries of the world. In such a developing economy a large proportion of the capital goods requirements must be imported and it is entirely possible that a domestic steel industry, even though its costs, and consequently its prices, may be higher than those of steel-exporting countries, may afford savings in foreign exchange. In other words, if domestic steel users purchase their steel requirements from home producers, that amount of foreign exchange that would have been spent on steel can be used to import other items. Yet these other items may of necessity include inputs to be used by the domestic steel industry; therefore, it cannot be assumed that each ton of domestically produced steel will save an amount of foreign exchange equal to the cost of importing a ton of foreign steel.

If all of the raw materials are found to be locally available and if all labor can be provided by nationals and if the capital equipment could be produced locally at the behest of domestic entrepreneurs using domestically held funds, the consumption of domestically produced steel would involve no loss of foreign exchange. However, it is beyond the realm of probability that an underdeveloped economy could supply itself with all of the necessary inputs required to produce steel. This deficiency is especially true of the immense and intricate capital equipment required for a steel mill. If the steel industry is either nonexistent or very small, it is very unlikely that there will be present the heavy machinery and metalworking industries necessary to produce the required capital goods, to say nothing of the wide technical knowledge required. Therefore, it can be concluded that most of the capital goods requirements will have to be met with imports and this obviously will affect the foreign exchange reserves position of the country. If foreign financing is obtained, the drain on foreign exchange will occur with each periodic payment, but whether the total cost or periodic payments are considered, the foreign exchange reserves will probably be tapped.

Further, if all or part of the raw materials must be imported, additional use will have to be made of foreign exchange reserves. The same applies to payments to technicians and skilled labor that may be imported (that part of the payroll going to foreigners that is not spent locally). This point can be made more clearly by employing the following equation for determining the size of the foreign exchange savings to be obtained from import substitution:

$$X = M - (Cm + Rm + Lm + Tf + Pf + Fm)$$

Where:

$X =$ Amount of foreign exchange savings
$M =$ Cost of total product if imported
$Cm =$ Cost of imported capital to produce product
$Rm =$ Cost of imported raw materials to produce product

Lm = Cost of imported labor required to produce product (this refers only to that amount which the imported workers remove from the country in which they are employed)

Tf = Transport costs paid to foreigners to haul imported capital goods, raw materials, or fuel

Pf = Profits distributed to foreigners

Fm = Cost of imported fuel required to produce the product

Cost of the product if imported (M) is used in the equation rather than the cost of the product if domestically produced, since the latter would cause the equation to give the amount of value added by manufacturing that is attributable to domestic factors. This would mean that if the domestic price were used, X would reflect foreign exchange savings only when the domestic price and the import price happened to be equal.

In the use of the term Cm (imported capital goods) there is the difficulty of specifying the time period in which the payments actually involve an outflow of funds. If financing is through a foreign bank, payments would be made by installments over a specified time period and each payment would constitute a claim against foreign exchange reserves. However, if financing were through a domestic bank, a lump sum payment would probably go from the bank to the foreign exporter or exporters and this payment would constitute the claim on foreign exchange. To complicate the picture further, the investment may be made by foreign entrepreneurs and, if so, the purchase would probably be made with funds held in foreign banks and the shipment of the plant and equipment would represent a transfer of real wealth but would involve no loss of foreign exchange. If the foreign entrepreneurs tapped funds which they had on deposit in the country in which they are investing, a drain on foreign exchange reserves would then be necessitated by the importation of the capital goods. In this case the drain on foreign exchange would come later and is comprehended within the term Pf, profits distributed to foreigners.

The significance of Rm, the cost of imported raw materials, is self-explanatory and Tf, the transport cost paid to foreigners, would cover the amount paid to transport the raw materials and capital equipment. Tf is separated from the cost of the items transported, as the hauling may occur by means of domestically owned conveyance as well as or instead of foreign-owned transport.

To quantify the term M, the time period used to limit the equation must be determined—say, one year's production or one ton of steel. To that quantity must be applied the import price or prices that would have been paid if the steel had been imported. All of the cost factors in the equation cover costs involved in manufacturing that quantity of steel subsumed under the term M.

The value of X rises as the total value of the factors Cm, Rm, Lm, Tf, Pf, and Fm decrease, so that the more of the cost of production attributed to domestic factors, the greater will be the foreign exchange savings. If 40 per cent of the value of the final product is accounted for by payments to domestic factors, the savings in foreign exchange will be equal to the cost of importing a given quantity of steel less the 60 per cent of the cost of production paid to foreign factors. This analysis makes what seems to be a valid assumption, that the cost of imported steel involves no significant payments to factors located in the underdeveloped country in question. As in the case of Venezuela, which exports large quantities of iron ore, the imported steel may contain ore that was originally from Venezuela, and in that case some of the loss of foreign exchange due to payment for the steel would be offset by the gain in foreign exchange from the iron ore exported to be used as an input in the imported steel.

Hypothetical cost data can supply meaning to the equation. Table 12 gives the payments to foreign factors for the various plants in Latin America.

Table 13 gives the costs for delivery of steel produced in the United States at Sparrows Point to the countries indicated.

Using the data in Table 12 and Table 13, the equation can be quantified to determine the amount of foreign exchange to be derived from the substitution of domestically produced steel for steel imports in the various Latin American countries having a domestic steel industry. The source material for the cost data in Table 12 does not tell how transportation has been considered; however, for purposes of exposition it will be assumed that such costs are subsumed under the heading "Sundry Expenses." It is further assumed that Sundry Expenses can be divided equally between transportation costs and profits distributed to foreigners.

To determine the per-ton savings in foreign exchange derived from the substitution of one ton of steel produced in Monclova for a ton of steel that would have been imported from Sparrows Point, the equation can be quantified as follows:

$$X = \$84.00 - (24.89 + 1.31 + 0.34 + 1.89 + 1.89)$$
$$X = \$53.68$$

Where:

$\$24.89 =$ Capital charges

$1.31 =$ Cost of imported raw materials

$0.34 =$ Cost of imported labor

$1.89 =$ Transportation costs

$1.89 =$ Profits distributed to foreigners

Thus $53.68 is the amount of foreign exchange that is saved by Mexico for every ton of Monclova steel that can be substituted for Sparrows Point steel.

For the other countries listed in Table 13, the following foreign exchange savings would be realized:

Argentina:

$$X = \$91.00 - (23.47 + 1.27 + 23.28 + 0.34 + 1.815$$
$$+ 1.815)$$
$$X = \$39.01$$

Brazil:

$$X = \$86.00 - (23.14 + 1.04 + 12.84 + 0.31 + 1.735$$
$$+ 1.735)$$
$$X = \$45.20$$

Chile:

$$X = \$87.00 - (27.97 + 1.28 + 3.07 + 0.43 + 1.725$$
$$+ 1.725)$$
$$X = \$50.80$$

Colombia (250,000 tons capacity):

$$X = \$84.00 - (28.47 + 0.93 + 0.52 + 2.165 + 2.165)$$
$$X = \$49.75$$

Colombia (105,000 tons capacity):

$$X = \$84.00 - (27.33 + 1.12 + 0.52 + 2.485 + 2.485)$$
$$X = \$50.06$$

Venezuela (50,000 tons capacity):

$$X = \$82.00 - (33.15 + 1.53 + 3.11 + 0.78 + 3.10$$
$$+ 3.10)$$
$$X = \$37.23$$

Venezuela (150,000 tons capacity):

$$X = \$82.00 - (31.56 + 1.15 + 3.11 + 0.47 + 2.42$$
$$+ 2.42)$$
$$X = \$40.87$$

TABLE 12

Payments to Foreign Factors[a]

(In U.S. Dollars at 1948 Costs Per Ton of Steel Ingots)

Plant	Imported Fuel	Wages and Salaries	Ferro Alloys	Sundry Expenses	Capital Charges	Total Payments to Foreign Factors
San Nicolás (Argentina)	23.28	0.34	1.27	3.63	23.47	51.99
Volta Redonda (Brazil)	12.84	0.31	1.04	3.47	23.14	40.80
Huachipato (Chile)	3.07	0.52	1.28	3.55	27.97	36.30
Belencito						
(250,000)	.....	0.52	0.93	4.33	28.47	34.25
(105,000)	.....	0.52	1.12	4.97	27.33	33.94
Monclova (México)	.....	0.34	1.31	3.78	24.89	30.32
Chimbote						
(50,000)	3.11	0.78	1.53	6.20	33.15	44.77
(150,000)	3.11	0.47	1.15	4.84	31.56	41.13

Source: United Nations, *A Study of the Iron and Steel Industry in Latin America.*
[a] Based upon hypothetical cost data.

TABLE 13

Cost of Imported Steel (1948)
(U.S. Dollars)

Country	Cost per Ton
Argentina	91.00
Brazil	86.00
Chile	87.00
Colombia	84.00
Mexico	84.00
Venezuela	82.00

Source: United Nations, *A Study of the Iron and Steel Industry in Latin America*, I.

One might suppose that the difference in foreign exchange savings between these two sizes of plants in Venezuela derives from economies of scale; the difference in cost here observed will be significant for the discussion of economies of scale in the next chapter. It should now be apparent that the amount of foreign exchange savings derived from import substitution of domestic steel for foreign steel varies from country to country and if the impact on the balance of payments is to be a consideration taken into account when deciding whether or not to have a domestic steel industry, one must go beyond the total cost figures and analyze the factors of production individually. Here it should be recalled that the method of analysis presented above is not intended as a measure of the impact on the balance of payments of an import replacement policy for any given industry, but is for the more limited purpose of measuring the amount of foreign exchange savings per unit of output.

A glance at Table 12 tells that most of the difference in "Total Payments to Foreign Factors" is made up of the cost of imported fuel. For example, while Mexico has no loss of foreign exchange due to imports of fuel, Argentina pays out $23.28 in foreign exchange for each ton of finished steel produced. It is not inconceivable that a situation might arise where a domestic steel industry would afford very little exchange savings. This could be the case for Central America, where proposals for an integrated steel industry have been studied.[1] In this case the market would be very small and thus capital charges would probably be larger than any of those here studied.[2] Also, a scarcity of coking coal might necessitate imports of fuel if the "classic" process of ore reduction is used. Further, the domestic reserves of iron ore may not be sufficient in Central America to carry the industry for more than several decades and this may mean that importation of iron ore would become necessary.[3]

It would be possible to have a situation in which payments to foreign factors approached or even exceeded the cost of importing the steel, as in the case of a highly inefficient operation in which capital costs were excessive because of low utilization of capacity. In a situation where capital goods are imported, where investment is made by foreigners or financed through foreign institutions, and where raw materials must be imported, the only significant domestic factor is labor (minus that pay to foreign technicians which does not remain in the country). When raw materials and fuel are imported, the volume of imports measured in tons will be larger than the volume of imported steel equal to the amount of steel produced by the imported raw materials because, as pointed out earlier, several tons of ore are required for the production of one ton of finished steel.

Pursuing this situation further, the percentage of total cost paid to labor is likely to be found to be small. While in the United States steel industry, employment costs account for 38.9 per cent of total cost, in Mexico these costs amount to only 11.7 per cent of the total.[4] It may be concluded that under the hypothetical situation as defined (higher transportation and capital costs, the cost of imported fuel and ore, and lower labor costs for the domestic industry as compared to the United States), the foreign exchange savings might be very small if not nonexistent. For the Mexican case, however, these savings are significant. Yet it is important to remember that,

[1] United Nations, *Possibilities of Integrated Industrial Development in Central America*, pp. 1–12.

[2] *Ibid.*

[3] *Ibid.*, p. 5. The extent of Central American iron ore reserves has not been fully determined. Small reserves have been located in Costa Rica and Nicaragua and a larger reserve of eight to ten million tons in Honduras. These reserves prove to be 53 per cent ore; they will afford no more than fifteen to twenty years of supply for steel production (assuming consumption at about 200,000 tons per year).

[4] Altos Hornos de México, S.A., *Informe Anual 1960.*

even in Mexico's case, the foreign exchange savings deriving from import substitution are significantly less than would be surmised from computations based solely on import costs without consideration of the cost of imported inputs on the part of the domestic steel industry.

In choosing between competing industrial investments and in a setting where foreign exchange savings is one of the goals of an import replacement policy, this type of analysis may help to determine the amount of foreign exchange savings *per unit* of domestic product substituted for a comparable import. The level of exchange savings will then depend on the number of units involved in the substitution. This determination is outside the scope of this chapter, but would possibly be determined by projection of consumption trends, with allowance for the impact of the proposed investment upon the economy in general.

4. Forward Linkages and the Price Effects of Import Substitution

The steel industry is linked in both backward and forward directions to a great number of other industries. The concept of backward linkage as expounded by Hirschman refers to the derived-demand effect of every "nonprimary activity."[1] This is to say that every nonprimary productive activity involves the use of some inputs from some other industry or industries. The inducement that is given to domestic entrepreneurs (either public or private) to supply these inputs through domestic production is the backward-linkage effect. This concept will be dealt with extensively in Chapter 7.

Forward linkage implies that every industry "that does not by its nature cater exclusively to final demands, will induce attempts to utilize its outputs as inputs in some new activities."[2] As an example, Hirschman cites the stimulating effect of a domestic iron and steel industry on the industries that use steel as inputs.

In discussing linkage effects and the steel industry, we will see that not only does the industry itself have backward- and forward-linkage effects upon other industries, but the forward-linkage effects of the primary product industries (iron ore, coal, etc.) and the backward-linkage effects of the industries that use steel as inputs may be decisive in determining whether or not there will be, in fact, a steel industry and, once established, what the level of production will be. It can be said with certainty that without the backward-linkage effects of the steel-using sectors, there would be no inducement to establish a steel industry. An extreme example of this type

[1] Albert O. Hirschman, *The Strategy of Economic Development*, p. 100.
[2] *Ibid.*

of linkage inducement at work can be found in the Mexican experience. What is today Mexico's third largest integrated steel company, Hojalata y Lámina, S.A., was established in Monterrey for the primary purpose of supplying flat-rolled steel to Fábricas Monterrey, S.A., which in turn used the steel to make crown corks, principally for a large Monterrey brewery.[3] Today we see that this company which was established in response to a demand ultimately derived from the level of beer consumption has grown to the extent that its production in 1961 was 381,000 tons of steel. Thus the linkage concept must be viewed as a two-edged sword. Forward linkage for the steel industry constitutes backward linkage for the industries using steel as an input. That is simply to say that the same production of finished goods that is considered to be induced by the establishment of a steel industry can be looked upon as the backward linkage of the steel-using industries which should, in and of itself, have inducement effects toward the establishment of steel-producing capacity.

As a technological concept, the forward linkage between the steel mill and steel-using industries is obvious; however, when one attempts to give an economic meaning to linkages, their nature is somewhat obscure. Is it to be assumed that the mere fact of the existence of a domestic steel industry will induce additional use of steel as inputs by the steel-using sectors above and beyond that amount of steel that would have been imported? In the first place, the substitution of the domestic product for imported steel will not be automatic, unless it is assumed that national pride will somehow transcend the profit motive. While the use of theoretical tools may tend to oversimplify the picture, the use of comparative prices and demand elasticity as a means of understanding the inducement effect of forward linkages may prove rewarding. In the first place, to speak of forward-linkage inducement effects without considering the relative prices of domestic and imported goods would seem to rule out a major factor, especially in the steel industry, as countries with major steel industries are located around the world from Eurupe to the Orient and steel in all shapes, sizes, and qualities can be imported by any underdeveloped country. If the possibility of "domophobia"[4] is overlooked and such factors as service and sales-

[3] Vargillo Garza, Jr., "Brief Sketch of the Industrial Development of Monterrey," in Basic Industries in Texas and Northern Mexico, p. 103.
[4] Hirschman, Strategy of Economic Development, p. 125. Hirschman defines "domophobia" as the fear of domestic goods which he says is found in under-

TABLE 14

Comparative Prices of Steel Products[a]
(In Mexican Currency Per Ton)

	AHMSA	Pittsburgh
Plate	445.40	411.56
Sheet	445.40	364.02

Source: Oscar Realme Rodríguez, "La Industria Siderúrgica Nacional."
[a] Delivered to Mexico City, including tariff on imports.

manship are held constant, the decision as to whether to use domestic or imported steel will turn on price. Price in both cases will be considered to include transportation costs to deliver the product to the purchaser. Thus, assuming that the government imposes no tariff on the importation of steel, if the prices quoted by a new domestic mill are lower than import prices, the inducement effect of domestic steel will depend upon the elasticity of demand for the steel. In other words, if the steel products in question have a high price elasticity of demand, the forward-linkage inducement effects will be great and if the elasticity coefficient is low, the inducement effects will be small.

A not unlikely situation is one where domestic prices for steel are higher than import prices, as was the case in Mexico during much of the decade following the establishment of AHMSA (see Table 14). In such a case, unless demand is perfectly inelastic, the effect of import substitution will be a tendency to deter the growth of the steel-using industries, such as the steel-fabricating mills that incorporate steel as a part of a finished product and those industries that include construction, whose demand for steel is a "final" demand. It is concluded that a government policy of implementing import substitution by way of tariffs would tend to have, in this case, a deleterious effect upon the growth of those industries using steel as an input. If "rational" economic behavior (in terms of price) is assumed, this substitution would have to be forced by the use of commercial policy tools on the part of the government.

Even though the demand for steel as an industrial input is a derived demand, ultimately depending, in many cases, on consumer

developed countries. It is somehow feared that the domestic producer cannot match the quality of the producer in the more industrialized countries.

demand for the products in which steel has been incorporated, one would probably want to assume that demand for steel would have an elasticity coefficient larger than zero. This being the case, the so-called inducement effects of the substitution of domestic steel for imported steel can be graphically illustrated (see Figure 4).

DD represents the demand of steel-using industries for steel at various prices, *P*. If *Pd* and *Pm* represent, respectively, domestic price and import price of identical steel products, and if *Xd* and *Xm* represent, respectively, the quantity of domestically produced steel and imported steel that would be purchased at various prices, the inducement or retarding effect of substituting domestic steel for imported steel can be illustrated. As before, all other factors are held constant.

If, with the import price at *Pm*, the price of domestically produced steel is Pd_3, the maximum amount of steel that would be purchased would be measured by *OXm* and the steel-using industries

FIGURE 4

Price Effects of Import Substitution

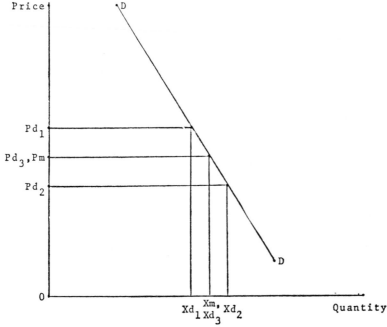

would be indifferent as to the source of their supply. Again, both prices are defined to include transportation costs, so that, in effect, delivery price to the consumer is being used. In the event that government policy excluded import of the steel product in question, the distance OXm would measure the maximum that would be purchased from domestic suppliers.

However, if the domestic price is located at Pd_2, the maximum market would be measured by the distance OXd_2 and all of the product in question would be supplied by the domestic producer or producers (this, of course, assumes that the domestic producer has sufficient capacity to supply that quantity). Since the distance OXd_2 is greater than the distance OXm, it may be inferred that the existence of a domestic steel industry had a positive-inducement effect upon the steel-consuming industries and that the magnitude of this effect can be measured by the distance $XmXd_2$. However, the reverse effect would occur if, with the import price at Pm, the domestic price were located at Pd_1. In this case the maximum market for the steel, in a no-tariff situation, would be measured by the distance OXm and the total supply would be imported. If sufficient protection were given to exclude foreign suppliers, the market for the domestic product would be measured by the distance OXd_1. Here it is observed that the substitution of a domestic product for imports has a retarding effect upon the consumption of the product, the magnitude of the retarding effects is represented by the distance $XmXd_1$.

Although the relative magnitudes of gain and loss would vary with changes in the slope of the demand curve, this analysis is valid for showing the tendency of relative prices to affect consumption of steel when demand for steel can be represented by any negative slope up to perfect inelasticity.

In the Mexican experience the prices for domestic steel were higher than the prices for imported steel immediately following the establishment of AHMSA. The prices listed in Table 14, for example, show the discrepancy between the cost of Pittsburgh steel and Monclova steel.

Given the data in Table 14, one would conclude that if, as would seem logical, the demand for the steel products listed was somewhat more elastic than perfect inelasticity, the effect of having to use domestic steel plate or sheet would be a tendency toward the reduction of the level of consumption of these products below that which would have been forthcoming if imported steel could have been used.

A look at the tariff schedules in Chapter 2 shows that in 1946 the tariff on steel plate was raised from .03 pesos per gross kilogram to .10 pesos plus 30 per cent ad valorem, thereby giving protection to the "high-cost" domestic product. Also, an examination of Figure 1, Chapter 2, indicates that the tariff policy probably had a major impact on imports of steel plate, for the level of imports declined from 40,724 tons in 1946, the year prior to the increase in the tariff, to 16,075 tons in 1947 and 7,864 tons in 1948. Consumption figures show that in 1946, 85,960 tons of steel plate were consumed in Mexico and that the level of consumption fell to 68,715 tons in 1947 and to 53,904 tons in 1948 (data in Table 23). Admittedly, factors other than price must have played important roles; however, it would seem logical to attribute some of the decline in consumption to price effects. If the price of the cheaper imports had not been raised by the tariff increase, a higher level of consumption of steel plate might have been encouraged.

Possible effects of price upon consumption have been referred to as "tendencies." These effects cannot be measured, even with a model that would hold constant all factors except price and demand, because a demand curve cannot be statistically derived. However, if it were determined that in some industries producing products containing a high percentage of steel, changes in demand for steel would in some measure vary inversely with price changes, the existence of these tendencies could be acknowledged even though they could not be measured. There are many factors other than price which influence the demand for steel; therefore, it cannot be said that any change in quantity demanded which occurs in conjunction with a price change was caused by that price change. Secondary effects and general equilibrium implications are involved in the investment in a domestic steel industry. Secondary effects would include the additions to income and employment by the backward-linkage industries, such as iron ore and coal, which were called into production by the domestic steel industry. Further, the investment in the steel industry would effect the general equilibrium via the investment multiplier. Subsequent increases in national income would tend to raise the level of demand for steel, the magnitude of which would be determined by the income elasticity of demand for steel products.

It may very well be that the "tendency" of price to affect demand would either be overcome or bolstered by the secondary and general equilibrium effects.

Nevertheless, the planner investigating the efficacy of establishing a high cost domestic steel industry may want to reverse his telescope so as to take some micro views of that industry's economic impact. An example might be the impact of a high-cost steel industry upon the output of a railcar manufacturer. Since steel is the major input, costs of railcar production would reflect the difference in price between high-priced domestic steel and low-priced imported steel, if import substitution were forced. And, if as in the case of Mexico's Constructora Nacional de Carros de Ferrocarril, S.A., a significant amount of the cars are intended for the export market, price increases could affect output and hence consumption of steel plate. Although the price effects cannot be measured, it should be kept in mind that they may have an impact on certain steel-using industries. If the adverse price differential is going to be great, and if the differential is expected to continue over a long period of time, the planner may want to give added weight to consideration of using other industries to effect import substitution.

However, it may be that the adverse price differential will be expected to decrease if projected production increases effect economies of scale. Short-run adverse price effects might give way to long-run price advantage for the domestic industry. As noted in Chapter 3, this has been the case in Mexico with regard to flat-rolled steel products. The long-run price advantage might also lead to exploitation of export markets, the impact of which would favorably affect balance of payments considerations. This also has been the Mexican case where, as outlined in Chapter 8, exports have increased to the point that in 1963, 177,181 tons of steel were exported, which earned 330,009,000 pesos in foreign exchange.[5]

Finally, if it is agreed that price has some inverse relationship with the level of consumption, an important rationale may have been found for advocating promotion of an infant steel industry by means of a production subsidy as opposed to tariff. The tariff is designed to raise the price of foreign goods with the intended result of replacing the imports with domestic products. In most cases the cost to the consumer of the domestic product is higher than the cost of the import minus tariff and according to the preceding analysis the

[5] Cámara Nacional de la Industria del Hierro y del Acero, *Circular No. 19.*

higher cost would exert a negative effect on the level of consumption. If, however, a production subsidy were selected as the tool for promoting an infant steel industry, the price of the domestic product might be lowered to the extent of being equal to world prices, in which case there would be no deleterious effects on steel consumption. If, on the other hand, the subsidy allowed the lowering of the domestic price to less than the world price, consumption of steel might be stimulated.

In this chapter and the preceding one the fact has been noted that economies of scale can effect both the level of foreign-exchange savings and the price of the product, therefore, it is appropriate that some consideration be given to the nature of those economies.

If price is to be considered as having an effect on the volume of steel consumption, industrial planners may want to concern themselves with determining what effect the size of the market will have upon the cost and consequently the price of the product produced. This concern would stem from the fact that steel is a high-capital-cost industry and consequently the lower the level of production, the greater the amount of capital cost to be attributed to each unit of output. Steel technology cannot be tailored to the size of market in such a way as to be efficient at low levels of production. Thus it might be expected that in countries with a low level of steel consumption, the per ton cost of steel production will be higher than the world price. As the size of the market increases, fuller use may be made of available steel technology so that at some level of production, if labor and/or raw materials can be had at a savings over world costs, the unit cost of domestic steel may fall below the world price of steel plus transportation costs. In addition to affecting the level of consumption via price, economies of scale, if realized among factors of production that require an outlay of foreign exchange, can affect the level of foreign exchange savings.

Figure 5 represents the impact of economies of scale upon total cost of steel production and upon the comparative costs of imported steel and domestic production.

The distance OL measures the cost of capital and maintenance that are fixed. That is to say that while zero units of imports have a cost of zero, the cost of zero units of domestic production is measured by the distance OL. The amount of fixed costs and consequently the origin and position of the Cd curve depend on the size of the plant the planners deem desirable for the country being considered. The

FIGURE 5

Total Cost with Economies of Scale

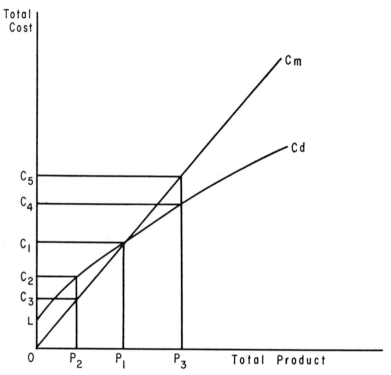

curved slope of the *Cd* curve indicates economies of scale as the level of production increases.

As more units of product are imported or produced locally, movement is made out along the horizontal axis or Total Product line and the total cost for that amount of product can be read off the vertical axis, or Total Cost line, so that for any point on the product axis, total cost of domestic production and total cost of imports can be read. For example, if domestic consumption of steel were equal to the distance, OP_2, the total cost, if all consumption were satisfied by domestic production, would be measured by the distance OC_2. However, if the same amount of steel were imported, the total cost would be less, and measured by OC_3 ($OC_3 < OC_2$). It would follow, of course, that the per unit costs would vary proportionately so that

$OC_3/OP_2 < OC_2/OP_2$. Only at OP_1 will cost of imports and cost of domestic production be equal.

The Cm curve will be a straight line out of the origin since the per unit price of imported steel can be taken as given regardless of the level of purchases, that is, one ton or one thousand tons would be valued at the same price per ton. (The likely assumption is made that the level of steel consumption in the underdeveloped country would not be sufficiently large to effect significant economies or diseconomies for the world steel industry, but the possibility is ignored that discounts may be given for purchases in large quantities). However, the sum of purchases by a country would not be based on one transaction, as the purchases are made by many different individuals and firms from many different producers in widely disparate areas, making it impossible to assess the impact, if any, of a quantity discount. The per unit cost of imports is therefore assumed to be an average of the purchase price of all of the individual transactions (weighted average).

Referring to the previous analysis of the effect of demand elasticity upon consumption, it might be said that if demand for steel is somewhat elastic (less than completely inelastic), at any level of production less than OP_1, the domestic price will be such that, if the domestic product is substituted for imports, the level of demand for steel will be somewhat curtailed. On the other hand, given the same degree of elasticity as above, if domestic production is at a level greater than OP_1, the demand for steel will be somewhat stimulated by the substitution of domestic steel for imports.

Diagrammed on a unit-cost basis, the same type of analysis can be made, as is shown in Figure 6.

The slope of the Cd curve depicts the "normal" situation of decreasing cost due to economies of scale (increasingly more efficient combinations of factors) and, finally, increasing costs due to diseconomies of scale.

Only at a production level of OP_1 are the price of imports and price of domestic production equal. While at product quantity OP_2, the price of imports remains OC_1, the unit cost of domestic production is greater as measured by OC_2. And when the market is sufficient to support a steel consumption of OP_3, the domestic price will be OC_3 which is less than the import price.

By analyzing cost data presented by the Economic Commission for Latin America, a schedule can be set up of hypothetical per unit

FIGURE 6

Unit Cost with Economies of Scale

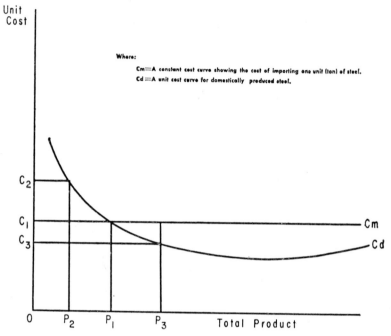

Where:

Cm=A constant cost curve showing the cost of importing one unit (ton) of steel.
Cd=A unit cost curve for domestically produced steel.

TABLE 15

Schedule of Hypothetical Unit Cost for Mexico's Monclova Plant
(1948 U.S. Dollars Per Ton)

Level of Production (Tons/Year)	Unit Cost
50,000	105.10
150,000	97.19
200,000	93.30
230,000	88.86
300,000	85.49
430,000	83.10
716,000	80.00
850,000	80.97

Source: Derived from data in United Nations, *A Study of the Iron and Steel Industry of Latin America*, Vol. I. For a description of the derivations, see Appendix A.

FIGURE 7

Hypothetical Unit Cost with Economies of Scale

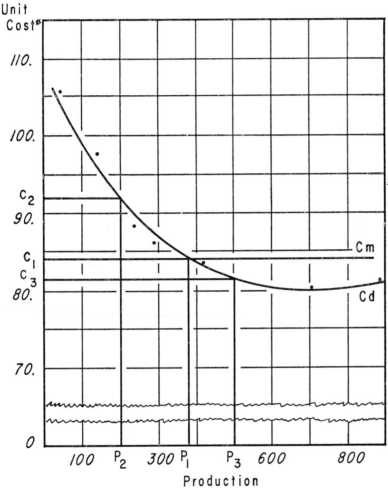

*dollars per metric ton

costs for Mexico's Monclova plant. Such a schedule is presented in Table 15.

The cost data are for the year 1948. For that year the price of steel imported from Sparrows Point was $84.00 per ton.[6] Figure 7

[6] United Nations, *A Study of the Iron and Steel Industry in Latin America*, p. 122.

FIGURE 8

Foreign Exchange Savings Curve

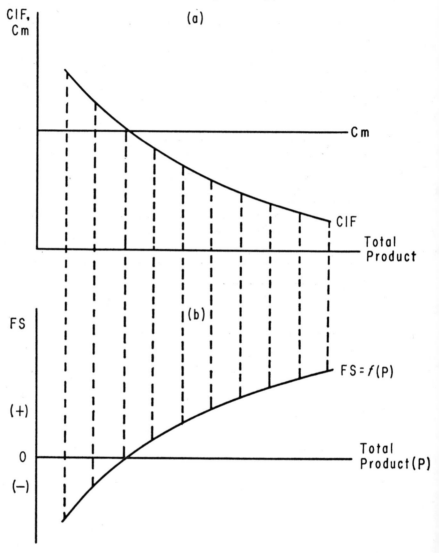

Cm=Cost of Imports (per ton)
CIF=Cost of Imported Factors (per ton of domestic steel)
FS=Foreign Exchange Savings (per ton of domestic steel)
P=Level of Production

shows that at a production level of 375,000 tons, the domestic industry can produce at $84.00 per ton, or a cost equal to the price of imports of Sparrows Point steel. If the level of production were less, the cost of domestic production would be $91.75 per ton, or $7.25 greater than the import price. If, on the other hand, production were at 500,000 tons, the domestic price would be less than the import price.

The level of production will have an impact upon the price of the steel products and the price, in turn, will probably have some effect upon the level of demand for the steel products. However, in addition to these influences, the economies of scale derived from the level of production will also determine the amount of foreign exchange savings to be obtained from each domestically produced unit which is substituted for imports. This is to say, that while the basic formula of Chapter 3 $(X = M - [Cm + Rm + Lm + Tf + Pf + Fm])$ tells at any given level of production what the foreign exchange savings will be, with economies of scale, it is the level of production that determines the amount of cost per unit to be attributed to the various factors making up that cost. This principle is illustrated in Figure 8. In Figure 8(a), the *CIF* curve is a cost curve for the per unit cost of factors of foreign origin. Included in this curve would be the per unit cost of imported capital goods, imported labor, and imported raw materials.

In Figure 8(b) the *FS* curve measures the per unit value of foreign exchange savings derived from substituting the domestic product for imports. The *FS* curve is the derivative of the *CIF* curve and for any level of production (P), a vertical line can be drawn up or down to the *FS* curve, from which point the amount of foreign exchange savings can be read on the vertical axis.

This is further illustrated in Figure 9, where data obtained from Table 70 (Appendix B) is plotted and a *CIF* curve and an *FS* curve are approximated from these points. In plotting the points in Figure 9(a), only capital charges were used. First, as described in Appendix B, cost data proportional to capacity changes were available for only capital and labor. Second, the amount of labor involving foreign exchange payments is less than 1 per cent of total cost while capital charges involving foreign exchange payments make up 81 per cent of payments to foreign factors. Thus, of necessity, it is assumed that the per unit costs of factors other than capital that require foreign exchange outlay do not vary with the level of production.

FIGURE 9

Hypothetical Foreign Exchange Savings

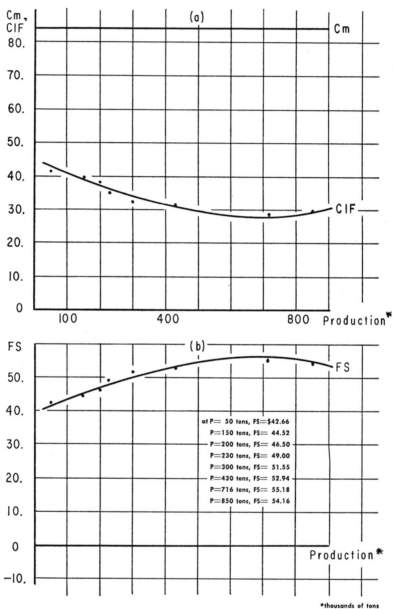

at P= 50 tons, FS=$42.66
P=150 tons, FS= 44.52
P=200 tons, FS= 46.50
P=230 tons, FS= 49.00
P=300 tons, FS= 51.55
P=430 tons, FS= 52.94
P=716 tons, FS= 55.18
P=850 tons, FS= 54.16

*thousands of tons

5. Production and Consumption:
The Forward Linkages
of the Steel Industry

This chapter includes an analysis of the trends of production and consumption during the recent past. Production and consumption data are presented first in aggregate form and then on the basis of product type. The data presented here will serve as a basis for some of the projections of consumption presented in Chapter 6.

Steel Production and Consumption
in the Aggregate

With the advent of World War II, the consumption of steel in Mexico began to grow at a rapid pace. The fact that the world's major manufacturing countries were included among the belligerents of that war meant that the traditional sources of steel and steel products were "dried up" to a large extent. Mexico, like other underdeveloped countries of the world, imported a large proportion of the steel consumed by her economy. For example, in 1940 the consumption of 258,793 tons of steel (in ingots) included 114,615 tons of imported steel. Imports accounted for about 40 per cent of steel consumed. While the war was curtailing the normal sources of supply of steel, it was affording an increased level of demand on the part of the industrialized countries for the primary products of the underdeveloped countries. These two factors, increased earnings from foreign trade by the underdeveloped countries and the curtailment of traditional sources of supply of steel and steel products, were probably instrumental in leading Mexico into what Carlos Prieto termed "the beginning of the second epoch of Mexico's iron and steel industry."[1] Steel consumption began a relatively steady annual growth in 1939 with the "take-off" for growth of consumption occurring in the early 1940's. The rate of growth of steel consumption for the period 1934–1942 was 2.6 per cent, while that for the period 1943–1951 was 9.8 per cent, or an increase in the rate of growth of 7.2 per cent.

Steel production has been growing at a faster rate than consumption. For the period 1939–1962, the annual rate of growth of steel production was 12.5 per cent as compared to 10.1 per cent for consumption. The higher growth rate for production is explained by the fact that over the period 1939–1962 the Mexican government has successfully promoted an import-substitution policy. Obviously, unless steel exports become a significant factor, as the physical level of production approaches that of consumption, the difference in

TABLE 16

Consumption of Steel in Mexico
(Ingots)

Year	Tons	Year	Tons
1934	228,700	1949	653,957
1935	248,400	1950	788,007
1936	260,600	1951	1,069,980
1937	367,700	1952	1,011,867
1938	174,500	1953	905,710
1939	258,793	1954	929,903
1940	276,144	1955	1,138,924
1941	312,092	1956	1,490,411
1942	299,091	1957	1,713,583
1943	356,739	1958	1,622,028
1944	535,799	1959	1,518,870
1945	580,212	1960	1,856,248
1946	680,100	1961	1,896,788
1947	749,346	1962	1,899,877
1948	577,363	1963	2,021,380

Sources: For 1934–1938, United Nations, *A Study of the Iron and Steel Industry of Latin America*, I, 84; for 1939–1959, Cámara Nacional de la Industria del Hierro y del Acero, *Tercer Congreso Nacional de la Industria Siderúrgica*, p. 68; for 1960–1963, Nacional Financiera, *Informe Anual, 1964*, p. 214.

[1] Carlos Prieto, "La Industria Siderúrgica," *México, 50 Años de Revolución*, I: *La Economía*, 217.

TABLE 17

Production of Steel in Mexico
(Ingots)

Year	Tons	Year	Tons
1934	114,000	1949	370,669
1935	134,300	1950	390,356
1936	129,500	1951	466,683
1937	185,000	1952	533,291
1938	108,100	1953	525,030
1939	144,178	1954	609,450
1940	149,414	1955	725,350
1941	144,084	1956	888,412
1942	172,627	1957	1,049,666
1943	166,012	1958	1,115,000
1944	174,766	1959	1,327,752
1945	229,993	1960	1,491,778
1946	258,259	1961	1,693,076
1947	290,668	1962	1,710,662
1948	291,282	1963	2,016,833

Sources: For 1934–1938, United Nations, *A Study of the Iron and Steel Industry of Latin America*, I, 86; for 1939–1959, Cámara Nacional de la Industria del Hierro y del Acero, *Tercer Congreso Nacional*, p. 68; for 1960–1963, Nacional Financiera, *Informe Anual*, 1964, p. 214.

growth rates will lessen. Since the early 1940's, production has been in a race, so to speak, to catch up with steel consumption. While production has not quite overtaken consumption, the gap has been narrowed to the point that in 1963 production equalled 99.78 per cent of consumption. The substitution of domestic steel for foreign steel has not been completed, however; for the year 1963, 158,070 tons of finished products were imported and 171,313 tons were exported.

Steel production during none of the years 1938 through 1944 reached the level of the 185,100 tons achieved in 1937. Steady growth of production began in 1945, coinciding with commencement of production by AHMSA. The long gestation period for a new steel mill or for the installation of the equipment necessary for a significant expansion of existing facilities accounts in part for the seemingly slow response of domestic steel production to the increased demand. Another delaying factor was the time necessary to make the decisions to invest and to locate the necessary funds and equipment.

Both the level of steel production and steel consumption are tied to the Gross National Product. For the period 1939–1961, steel production correlates highly with the GNP, the coefficient of correlation being .956 (for details see Appendix C, No. 1). When correlat-

TABLE 18

Indices of Gross National Product, Steel Production,
and Steel Consumption in Mexico
(1950 = 100)

Year	Gross National Product	Steel Production	Steel Consumption
1939	49.4	37	33
1940	49.9	38	35
1941	56.1	37	40
1942	63.5	44	38
1943	65.9	43	45
1944	71.5	45	68
1945	77.0	59	74
1946	82.1	66	86
1947	83.2	75	95
1948	86.9	75	73
1949	90.7	95	83
1950	100.0	100	100
1951	107.2	120	136
1952	108.4	137	128
1953	107.0	135	115
1954	115.2	156	118
1955	126.5	186	145
1956	134.9	228	189
1957	139.8	269	218
1958	146.0	286	206
1959	152.8	341	193
1960	161.4	395	244
1961	------	431	239

Sources: Production index compiled from data in Table 17 and consumption from Table 16. Gross National Product: Cámara Nacional de la Industria de la Construcción, *Memoria del Segundo Congreso Mexicano de la Industria de la Construcción*, II, 772, and Dirección General de Estadística, *Compendio Estadístico 1960*, p. 157.

ing steel consumption and GNP for the same period, the coefficient of correlation is again high, but significantly less than that for production and GNP, being .727 (Appendix C, No. 1). A large part of this difference is probably accounted for by the fact that the level of steel consumption fluctuates much more than either GNP or steel production. This fluctuation can be seen in Table 18, where the data for steel consumption, steel production, and Gross National Product have been converted to index numbers so that their trends may be observed in juxtaposition. In any year the difference between consumption and production is made up in the foreign trade sector so that a more violent jump or dip in consumption vis-à-vis production results in increases or decreases in imports. A shortage of foreign exchange may result in curtailment of steel imports but have no direct impact on the level of domestic steel production.

As a measure of steel's contribution to the economic welfare of the country the per capita steel consumption for the years 1939–1960 is shown in Table 19.

To show how Mexico's per capita steel consumption compared with that of several other countries in the world, comparative data are presented in Table 20 for both developed and underdeveloped countries.

TABLE 19

Per Capita Steel Consumption in Mexico
(Kilograms)

Year	Kilograms	Year	Kilograms
1939	13.3	1950	30.5
1940	13.9	1951	40.3
1941	15.3	1952	37.1
1942	14.3	1953	32.3
1943	16.7	1954	32.2
1944	24.4	1955	38.4
1945	25.7	1956	48.9
1946	29.3	1957	54.5
1947	31.5	1958	50.1
1948	23.6	1959	45.6
1949	26.0	1960	50.0

Source: Cámara Nacional de la Industria del Hierro y del Acero, *Tercer Congreso Nacional*, p. 68.

TABLE 20

Per Capita Steel Consumption in Selected Countries in 1958
(Kilograms)

Country	Per Capita Consumption
Brazil	31
Canada	316
Chile	67
China (mainland)	11
Colombia	11
France	314
Mexico	50
U.S.S.R.	266
United States	433
West Germany	377

Source: Carlos Prieto, "La Industria Siderúrgica," *México, 50 Años de Revolución*, I: *La Economía*, 223.

In Mexico, for the period 1939–1960, the annual rate of growth of per capita steel consumption has been 6.7 per cent. This rate will be noted to be below the rate of growth of aggregate steel consumption, which was 10.1 per cent. As aggregate steel consumption grows, the population base used to compute per capita consumption grows also.

If Mexico continues to be successful in promoting industrialization, the steel industry might be expected to grow considerably. A glance at Table 20 shows that per capita steel consumption in Mexico is well below that of any of the industrialized nations. It might then be expected that with continued industrialization steel production could grow considerably before reaching a plateau. If per capita steel consumption continues its present trend it would grow to 69 kilograms by 1970. This projection is obtained from the data in Table 19 by fitting the linear equation

$$y = 11.961 + 1.864x.$$

Heretofore in this chapter we have considered steel production in the aggregate and the data presented have been in terms of tons of steel ingots. More than one ton of steel ingots (approximately 1.333 tons) is required to produce a ton of finished steel; therefore, the amount of finished steel actually consumed as inputs by the steel-

TABLE 21

Shares of Production and Consumption by Finished Steel Products
(Metric Tons)

Product	Production 1953–1962	% of Total	Consumption 1953–1962	% of Total
Construction Rods	1,767,186	18.4	1,768,023	15.3
Other Rods	43,399	0.4	144,036	1.2
Commercial Shapes	928,715	9.7	946,377	8.2
Structural Shapes	513,165	5.3	583,813	5.0
Wire	842,217	8.8	984,722	8.5
Railway Material	182,329	1.9	1,039,662	9.0
Plate	981,537	10.2	1,043,858	9.0
Sheet	2,281,749	23.7	2,507,848	21.6
Tinplate	447,685	4.7	652,219	5.6
Pipe w/seam	839,455	8.7	835,717	7.2
Seamless Pipe	723,770	7.5	1,013,424	8.7
Foundry Pipe	63,254	0.6	73,520	0.6
Total	9,614,461	99.9[a]	11,593,219	99.9[a]

Source: Computed from consumption and production figures found in succeeding tables of this chapter.

[a] Does not add to 100 per cent because of rounding.

using sectors is less than the amounts presented in Tables 16 and 17. The following pages will present a breakdown of production and consumption by the major finished products.

Table 21 breaks down production and consumption by product and shows the share that each has enjoyed for the period 1953–1962.

For the period 1953–1962, the production of pipe with seam exceeded consumption by 3,838 tons, indicating a net export balance for this product. The production of construction rods fell short of consumption by less than a thousand tons and production of both steel plate and sheet steel closely approximated consumption of those items. Also, production of both structural shapes and commercial shapes was a high percentage of consumption.

Production and Consumption of Finished Steel Products

Sheet steel was the first flat-rolled product to be produced by the Mexican industry, the first production dating to 1941. The level of production was of little consequence until AHMSA began to produce sheet in 1946. Before this there had been little investment in rolling mills for flat-rolled products because of the dearth of fabricating industries that could incorporate such steel in finished manufactured goods. Wartime shortages of imported manufactured goods and of flat-rolled steel products combined to produce market conditions that augured well for domestic production of flat-rolled products.

Table 22, listing production and consumption data for sheet steel for the period 1939–1963, shows that production of sheet steel has been successful in its efforts to overtake consumption. In both 1962 and 1963, production exceeded consumption. The annual rate of growth of sheet-steel production for the period 1953–1962 was 12.8 per cent, while that of consumption was 10.2 per cent.

Further, it can be noted from Table 22 that the level of sheet-steel consumption for the year 1957 showed only slight gains over 1956 and then fell sharply in 1958. Production also fell off sharply in 1958. These movements accompanied a leveling off of the growth

TABLE 22

Production and Consumption of Sheet Steel in Mexico
(Tons)

Year	Production	Consumption	Year	Production	Consumption
1939	....	6,577	1952	91,832	113,582
1940	....	9,546	1953	98,833	120,770
1941	921	10,662	1954	123,241	137,048
1942	4,251	13,012	1955	170,266	182,362
1943	10,746	33,898	1956	213,975	271,964
1944	14,773	55,011	1957	263,122	281,718
1945	20,598	36,473	1958	209,181	218,943
1946	31,298	45,794	1959	238,020	242,760
1947	44,160	55,717	1960	309,334	323,308
1948	52,542	68,606	1961	328,448	336,945
1949	62,805	83,198	1962	327,329	316,967
1950	78,202	101,889	1963	385,434	287,550
1951	92,040	122,291			

Source: Data for 1941–1952: Cámara Nacional de la Industria del Hierro y del Acero, *Segundo Congreso Nacional de la Industria Siderúrgica*, p. 52; data for 1953–1962: Arturo Salcido M., *El Mercado del Acero en México*, p. 40; data for 1963: Nacional Financiera, S.A., *Informe Anual, 1964*, p. 204.

of Gross National Product. As previously mentioned there is a high correlation between Gross National Product and both steel consumption and steel production.

For the year 1956 consumption grew much more than production, with a consequent increase in imports. In the following year when growth of consumption slumped, the level of imports dropped and domestic steel continued to replace more and more of imports. Apparently, in 1956 the domestic industry could not expand production sufficiently to satisfy that year's level of demand. From data shown in Chapter 2, it appears that the cost of importing sheet steel was above the domestic price for the entire period of 1953–1962.

Steel plate was first produced in Mexico by AHMSA and the first year of production was 1944. Production for that year amounted to only 4,002 tons but expanded rapidly in succeeding years, so that by 1962 production equaled 95 per cent of consumption. Table 23 gives production and consumption data for the period 1939–1963.

For the period 1953–1962, the annual growth rate of consumption

TABLE 23

Consumption and Production of Steel Plate in Mexico
(Tons)

Year	Production	Consumption	Year	Production	Consumption
1939	....	25,989	1952	50,869	62,577
1940	....	26,103	1953	57,652	63,389
1941	....	25,815	1954	63,620	69,297
1942	....	16,556	1955	72,897	79,036
1943	....	26,159	1956	75,879	80,914
1944	4,002	38,878	1957	101,776	107,914
1945	32,548	71,746	1958	99,178	104,007
1946	38,219	85,960	1959	138,363	142,448
1947	46,226	68,715	1960	154,466	158,225
1948	41,131	53,904	1961	132,145	136,628
1949	40,587	56,255	1962	85,559	87,588
1950	36,425	51,281	1963	192,921	194,511
1951	39,328	56,512			

Sources: Data for 1941–1952: Cámara Nacional de la Industria del Hierro y del Acero, *Segundo Congreso Nacional*, p. 52; data for 1953–1962: Salcido M., *El Mercado del Acero en México*, p. 40; data for 1963: Nacional Financiera, S.A., *Informe Anual, 1964*, p. 204.

was 8.0 per cent, while that of production was higher, 11.3 per cent. Unlike sheet, foreign trade in plate maintained an import balance throughout the period, but the gap between consumption and production was narrowed.

The same general cyclical pattern was followed as with sheet steel, with slight declines in consumption of both in 1958; however, the declines in 1961–1962 were much greater in steel plate. One reason for this tremendous decline can be traced to the drop in the production of railcars from a total in 1961 of 2,274 cars to only 787 in 1962.[2] The company manufacturing railcars, Constructora Nacional de Carros de Ferrocarril, was in the process of retooling to diversify output so as to produce other product lines in addition to railcars.[3]

Tin plate was first produced in Mexico by AHMSA in 1946. In terms of tons of steel, tin plate has the smallest market of all of the flat-rolled products; nevertheless, production as a percentage of consumption is smaller for tin plate than it is for either sheet steel or steel plate. Table 24 gives both production and consumption of tin plate for the period 1939–1963.

As with both sheet and plate, the rate of growth of production was significantly higher than that of consumption. For the period 1953–1962, production grew at an annual rate of 18.2 per cent as compared to 7.5 per cent for consumption.

It will be noted that neither consumption nor production suffered from fluctuations as violent as those observed for sheet and plate. Especially noteworthy is the fact that consumption of both sheet and plate declined toward the end of the period studied; however, consumption of tin plate continued to grow through the last six years of the period without a downturn. It is probable that the reason for this lies in the nature of the major industries using tin plate as an input. Food containers and bottlecaps account for a significant proportion of tin plate consumption and cyclical fluctuations would probably exercise less impact upon these products as compared to the heavier flat-rolled products used in such sectors as transportation, machinery, and durables, where the impact of a decline in the general economic health is felt first and hardest.

Railway steel for track and maintenance of way occupies a unique position in the Mexican steel picture. While this category of steel

[2] Nacional Financiera, *Informe Anual, 1964*, p. 66.
[3] *Ibid.*, p. 66.

TABLE 24

Consumption and Production of Tinplate in Mexico
(Metric Tons)

Year	Production	Consumption	Year	Production	Consumption
1939	....	19,240	1951	13,671	34,340
1940	....	18,613	1952	13,015	35,599
1941	....	20,655	1953	19,180	35,388
1942	....	17,540	1954	24,334	34,555
1943	....	17,239	1955	24,517	44,626
1944	....	17,381	1956	29,854	59,189
1945	....	18,463	1957	33,268	49,882
1946	2,373	16,599	1958	53,725	56,908
1947	3,169	28,793	1959	60,432	61,471
1948	5,112	21,994	1960	62,044	64,481
1949	10,052	28,369	1961	67,758	69,966
1950	11,785	31,728	1962	72,573	76,629
			1963	85,424	89,504

Sources: Data for 1941–1952: Cámara Nacional de la Industria del Hierro y del Acero, *Segundo Congreso Nacional*, p. 52; data for 1953–1962: Salcido M., *El Mercado del Acero en México*, p. 40; data for 1963: Nacional Financiera, S.A., *Informe Anual, 1964*, p. 204.

accounted for 9.0 per cent of total steel consumption during the period 1953–1962, only 17.5 percent of that consumption was satisfied by domestic supply. Beginning with the first decade of this century, Fundidora has produced rails and spikes but the productive capacity has been augmented very little and, in fact, it will be noted from Table 25 that it has shown a declining trend in recent years. The milling facilities that make rails are also used for heavy structural shapes and capacity has been increasingly utilized for production of the latter, structural shapes carrying a higher profit ratio.[4] Also, much railway material is imported because of long-established credit channels for purchase of foreign steel and large credit lines still open for long-term credit.

It can be noted that consumption has fluctuated violently over the ten-year period. Since most of the consumption is derived from imports, changing conditions of supply can be ruled out as accounting

[4] United Nations, *A Study of the Iron and Steel Industry in Mexico*, pp. 438–439.

TABLE 25

Consumption and Production of Railway Steel in Mexico
(Tons)

Year	Production	Consumption	Year	Production	Consumption
1942	20,577	21,299	1953	23,489	162,301
1943	18,040	19,846	1954	20,302	34,170
1944	29,052	34,206	1955	20,571	151,907
1945	22,115	28,531	1956	30,414	194,022
1946	21,642	56,997	1957	21,275	238,578
1947	18,314	101,810	1958	9,234	170,242
1948	9,824	57,930	1959	13,902	19,852
1949	30,566	57,114	1960	23,126	191,744
1950	17,962	93,651	1961	11,256	80,544
1951	22,183	158,223	1962	8,760	112,359
1952	....	....	1963	16,830	....

Sources: Data for 1942–1951: United Nations, *A Study of the Iron and Steel Industry in Mexico*, II, 443; data for 1953–1962: Salcido M., *El Mercado del Acero en México*, p. 38; data for 1963: Nacional Financiera, S.A. *Informe Anual, 1964*, p. 204.

for the sharp dips and peaks from year to year. The fluctuating trend derives from the fact that only one industry accounts for all of the consumption and one firm within that industry is dominant (National Railways of Mexico). The fact that the dominant firm is owned by the federal government undoubtedly plays a significant role in the spacing and magnitude of the fluctuations. Political and economic conditions for the nation as a whole play a part in the decisions to start, stop, or delay railway expansion or renovation and maintenance projects. In a recession, it may be easier for the government to delay rail maintenance projects than to curtail expenditures in other areas. Also, since most of the rails and maintenance of way materials are imported, the level of foreign exchange earnings and balance of payments pressures will be a factor in determining the level of imports in any given period. A project to replace worn rails may be delayed until balance of payments pressures subside, with the scarce foreign exchange going to sectors considered to have a higher priority.

Construction rods have been produced for many decades in Mexico both by Fundidora and smaller nonintegrated mills. Fundidora's price book for 1912 lists several sizes of construction rods.[5] These shapes are quite often rolled from such items as scrap rails by small mills requiring relatively small investments; therefore, it should not be surprising that most consumption is satisfied by domestic production, as can be observed from the data presented in Table 26.

Production for the period 1953–1962 trailed very closely behind consumption for most years and during the three-year period of 1959–1961 it exceeded consumption. Both production and consumption showed a big drop in 1958 which corresponded with steel trends in general for Mexico and with the decline in the Gross National Product growth rate. This decline in consumption of construction rods also corresponded with a decline in construction. In 1958 the index of construction dropped from 146.1 to 143.7 (see Table 31). The fact that consumption of construction rods is tied to the construction industry means that both consumption and production of this item can be expected to fluctuate with changes in the volume of construction.

Commercial shapes and heavy structural shapes are both produced in Mexico in quantities that amount to a significant portion of consumption. Table 21 shows that for the period 1953–1962 production of commercial shapes totaled 928,715 tons and of heavy structural shapes 513,165 tons while consumption totaled 946,377 tons and 583,813 tons respectively.

Tables 27 and 28 give data for consumption and production of both items.

The trend of growth of structural shapes is slow compared to that of commercial shapes. For the period 1953–1962, the annual growth rate for consumption of commercial shapes was 10.8 per cent and the rate of growth of production was 11.2 per cent. The rates of growth for consumption and production of structural shapes were 2.1 per cent and 3.6 per cent respectively.

Pipe in many varieties and sizes is produced by a number of firms in Mexico. AHMSA, of the integrated mills, produces pipe, but two other producers are large in terms of output: Tubacero of Monterrey and TAMSA in Veracruz. Pipe has many and varied uses, so that consumption is not tied to the demand of one sector or a few buyers. Uses range from plumbing that accompanies building con-

[5] Compañía Fundidora de Fierro y Acero de Monterrey, S.A. Price Catalog, 1912.

TABLE 26

Production and Consumption of Construction Bars (Rods)
(Tons)

Year	Production	Consumption
1953	83,030	87,443
1954	95,481	99,223
1955	111,192	116,072
1956	158,893	162,105
1957	201,553	205,353
1958	175,328	177,472
1959	212,168	205,090
1960	228,485	218,884
1961	246,644	241,989
1962	254,392	254,447
1963	309,068	309,068[a]

Sources: Data for 1953–1962: Salcido M., *El Mercado del Acero en México*, p. 33; data for 1963: Nacional Financiera, S.A., *Informe Anual, 1964*, p. 204.
[a] Estimated.

TABLE 27

Production and Consumption of Commercial Shapes
(Metric Tons)

Year	Production	Consumption
1953	48,156	51,344
1954	57,502	59,736
1955	60,361	61,519
1956	85,332	86,724
1957	108,617	111,045
1958	102,277	104,310
1959	109,984	110,676
1960	110,642	112,451
1961	116,046	117,684
1962	129,798	130,888
1963	125,382	....

Sources: Consumption: Salcido M., *El Mercado del Acero en México*, p. 35; Production: Nacional Financiera, S.A., *Informe Anual, 1964*, p. 214.

TABLE 28

Production and Consumption of Structural Shapes
(Metric Tons)

Year	Production	Consumption
1953	40,394	53,147
1954	46,416	55,352
1955	45,744	50,374
1956	39,231	44,798
1957	51,542	61,252
1958	68,556	76,687
1959	61,123	63,891
1960	48,473	55,712
1961	61,386	67,941
1962	50,300	54,659
1963	60,628	85,518

Sources: Consumption: Salcido M., *El Mercado del Acero en México*, p. 35;
Production: Nacional Financiera, S.A., *Informe Anual, 1964*, p. 214.

struction, pipelines, drainage, oil well drilling, etc. Table 29 presents production and consumption for three general types of pipe produced in Mexico.

Although production of seamless pipe did not begin until 1954, by 1962 domestic production accounted for 93 per cent of its consumption. Tubos Acero de México, of Veracruz, initiated production of this item and accounts for all of its production. It will be noted from Table 29 that two years (1961–1962) showed significant export balances in foreign trade in pipe with seam. In 1955 pipe produced by TAMSA received the approval of the American Petroleum Institute and subsequently the company has been able to export some pipe to the United States.[6] This pipe is generally of large diameter and is used mainly for pipelines and irrigation, with some smaller volume of consumption accounted for by electricity-generating facilities.[7] The principal purchasers of this pipe are governmental institutions, namely, Petroleos Mexicanos, the Secretary of Agriculture and Cattle, and the Federal Electricity Commission.

As of 1953, ten companies were devoted to the manufacture of

[6] Wolfgang Friedman and G. Kalmanoff, *Joint International Business Ventures*, p. 373.
[7] Arturo del Castillo, *Tubería Soldada de Gran Diámetro*, p. 13.

TABLE 29

Production and Consumption of Pipe in Mexico
(Metric Tons)

Year	Seamless		W/Seam		Foundry	
	Pro-duction	Con-sumption	Pro-duction	Con-sumption	Pro-duction	Con-sumption
1953	....	41,023	42,472	46,204	7,138	8,270
1954	5,352	87,237	51,438	55,266	9,742	12,483
1955	35,866	80,417	42,930	47,209	13,257	13,593
1956	49,664	78,932	37,218	42,290	9,006	10,139
1957	73,058	97,943	108,160	105,589	5,705	6,815
1958	98,570	120,445	122,315	124,368	3,859	5,163
1959	108,872	114,081	91,486	92,358	4,798	5,356
1960	123,181	139,403	125,867	127,437	2,306	3,040
1961	109,043	124,230	123,912	113,067	4,797	5,151
1962	120,150	129,713	93,657	81,929	2,646	3,510
1963	127,140	....	146,336	....	....	....

Source: Production: Nacional Financiera, S.A., *Informe Anual, 1963*, p. 204; Consumption: Salcido M., *El Mercado del Acero en México*, p. 44.

pipe with seam. AHMSA was the only integrated mill; therefore the others had to purchase the sheet steel and steel plate used as raw-material input from other firms.[8] Today TAMSA produces steel to use in its own pipe production. Flat-rolled steel accounts for approximately 97 per cent of the value of raw-material inputs for the manufacture of pipe with seam. As of 1950, the production of pipe accounted for 47 per cent of domestic production of steel plate, and, due to the shortage of this input, pipe manufacturers utilized only 30 per cent of capacity that year.[9] Increased domestic production of steel plate has worked to alleviate this shortage.

Foundry pipe is the only major item of steel that has shown a decline in both consumption and production. The annual rate of decline of consumption has been 14 per cent. For pipe with seam, the annual rate of growth of consumption has been 11.3 per cent and for seamless pipe, 10.8 per cent.

Wire is the last major finished-steel product to be considered. Steel wire has been produced for many decades. During the period

[8] *Ibid.*, p. 16.
[9] *Ibid.*, pp. 15, 36.

1953–1962 the level of production has closed the gap with consumption so that in 1963 domestic production equaled 97 per cent of wire consumed. Production and consumption data are presented in Table 32, from which an interesting phenomenon can be observed for 1955; in that year both consumption and production more than doubled. From Table 9, it can be noted that 1951 imports of wire were placed under quantitative restriction and could be made only with specific authorization of the Finance Minister. Likely these restrictions were inaugurated to protect and/or promote proposed increases in wiremaking capacity. In 1954 the tariff was raised from .05 pesos per kilogram plus 25 per cent ad valorem tax to .10 pesos plus 30 per cent ad valorem. The following year consumption fell as production rose somewhat, but in 1956, when production jumped markedly, suppressed demand rose also.

As mentioned at the beginning of this chapter, the data herein presented will be used to make projections as to the level of steel consumption in 1970.

TABLE 30

Production and Consumption of Steel Wire in Mexico
(Metric Tons)

Year	Production	Consumption
1953	22,583	44,755
1954	26,189	46,928
1955	28,490	39,257
1956	83,902	111,910
1957	97,919	102,691
1958	104,363	118,530
1959	108,178	115,752
1960	119,095	130,504
1961	127,998	135,613
1962	133,500	138,782
1963	136,414	141,132

Source: Production: Nacional Financiera, S.A., *Informe Anual, 1963*, p. 204; Nacional Financiera, S.A., *Informe Anual, 1964*, p. 214. Consumption: Salcido M., *El Mercado del Acero en México*, p. 36.

6. Steel Consumption
by Industrial Sector
and Projections for 1970

The first part of this chapter will be devoted to an analysis of steel consumption from the point of view of the consuming sectors: manufacturing, mining, agriculture, construction, petroleum, and transportation. The remainder of the chapter will be devoted to projections of steel consumption for the year 1970.

It was noted in Chapter 5 that consumption of steel in Mexico correlates highly with Gross National Product; the coefficient of correlation for the period 1939–1961 was .727. It might be suspected that the correlation coefficient for steel consumption and the index of industrial production would be even higher, and this is the case, as the coefficient for the period 1953–1961 is .93795 (see Appendix C, No. 3, for details of computation.)

The index of industrial production is shown in Table 31, together with indices for mineral, petroleum, construction, and manufacturing production.

As shown, the growth of steel consumption correlated highly with the growth of the index of industrial production and it might further be expected that growth of steel consumption by sectors would correlate highly with the growth of production in each sector. This hypothesis can be tested by correlating the series for each sector in Table 32 with its corresponding series in Table 31.

In comparing the index series for industrial production with that for total steel consumption, it becomes clear that steel consumption has grown at a faster rate than industrial production, which would indicate that the proportion of steel per unit of industrial output is growing. However, since steel is also consumed in other sectors, such as agriculture and public works, this inference cannot be justified

TABLE 31

Index of Industrial Production and Production Indices by Sectors
(1953 = 100)

Year	I.I.P.	Mining	Petroleum	Construction	Manu-facturing
1953	100.0	100.0	100.0	100.0	100.0
1954	106.7	91.6	105.4	105.1	108.8
1955	118.6	99.1	121.5	115.9	120.8
1956	130.4	107.2	133.5	130.3	132.6
1957	139.7	111.3	147.7	146.1	141.0
1958	146.2	106.5	168.9	143.7	147.8
1959	157.6	107.3	196.9	150.0	158.7
1960	170.8	110.6	209.7	169.0	172.4
1961	178.5	107.1	241.4	171.2	178.4

Source: Computed from data in Nacional Financiera, S.A., *Estadísticas Económicas de México.*

from global consumption data. It can, however, be determined from the sectoral data if the growth has been true on a sector basis.

A correlation of manufacturing production with steel consump-

TABLE 32

Indices of Steel Consumption by Sectors
(1953 = 100)

Year	Total Steel Consumption	Mining	Petroleum	Construction	Manu-facturing
1953	100.0	100.0	100.0	100.0	100.0
1954	102.8	84.8	130.1	116.5	116.6
1955	125.9	125.2	132.9	125.7	133.3
1956	164.6	140.4	154.7	160.7	191.4
1957	189.4	158.3	210.7	204.3	180.6
1958	179.2	146.3	217.3	192.3	171.2
1959	167.8	112.8	207.2	203.8	198.6
1960	212.8	140.5	206.4	226.6	234.2
1961	208.5	134.0	187.3	243.6	234.7

Sources: Sectoral indices derived from data in Arturo Salcido Moreneau, *El Mercado del Acero en México*, p. 45; index for "Total Steel Consumption" derived from data in Table 16, Chapter 5.

tion by the manufacturing sector yields a coefficient of .962 (see Appendix C, Nos. 4–7, for details of correlation). Thus, steel would seem to be an important input for manufacturing in general. Tables 31 and 32 reveal that consumption of steel by the manufacturing sector has grown significantly more rapidly than production by that sector. For the mining sector, the coefficient of correlation between mining production and steel consumption by that sector is .849, which indicates that changes in mining output entail significant changes in steel consumption (see Appendix C, Nos. 4–7). The coefficient of correlation for the index of construction and the consumption of steel by that sector is the highest of all sectors, .991 (Appendix C, Nos. 4–7). It is also indicated in Tables 31 and 32 that steel consumption has grown faster than output for the construction sector. The lowest correlation between output and steel consumption is found in the petroleum sector, where the coefficient is .748 (Appendix C, Nos. 4–7). It will also be noted that by 1961, the index of petroleum production had outstripped that of steel consumption for the petroleum sector, but this was not true of all of the preceding years covered by the index.

A method for measuring the rate of increase of steel consumption per unit of added output for each of the sectors can be found in regression analysis. If a sectoral steel-consumption index is regressed on the production index for that sector, the B coefficient will give the rate of change in "steel intensiveness." From the equations located in Appendix C (Nos. 4–7), the following B coefficients have been taken:

Manufacturing 1.707
Mining 3.149
Construction 1.962
Petroleum .... .656

From these coefficients we learn that during the period 1953–1961, for every increase of one index number point in manufacturing production, consumption of steel by the manufacturing sector increased by 1.707 index number points. A one-point increase in output led to an increase in steel use of 3.149 index number points in mining, 1.962 points in construction, and .656 point in petroleum. An increase is thereby indicated in the technical-linkage tie between the steel industry and each of the consuming sectors except petroleum. Only in petroleum did a given percentage increase in production lead to a higher percentage increase in steel consumption. The decline would indicate that over the period 1953–1961 the petroleum industry became less steel-intensive.

The preceding analysis indicates an overall increase in the linkage dependency of manufacturing, construction, and mining upon the steel industry. Yet although these sectors have become more steel-intensive, no precise measure can be given as to how much of this was due to the fact that there was a domestic steel industry. That current levels of steel consumption could have been supported by imports is doubtful, however, as pointed out in Chapter 8. The sure supply of domestic steel as compared to the foreign market with its vagaries of balance of payments positions must have had some positive effect upon decisions to invest in the industrial sectors.

In Figures 10, 11, 12, 13 the consumption data in Table 33 have been plotted to semi-log scale and trend lines have been fitted so that projections of consumption can be made. In some cases both linear trend lines and semi-log trend lines have been fitted to the same data. This is the case with agricultural and construction steel consumption. In these cases there was some doubt as to which would have the better fit. The linear trend line would produce a straight line if plotted to arithmetic scale, but since such a line indicates a declining growth rate it would have a diminishing slope when plotted on semi-log paper. The equations for the projections are found in Tables 34 and 35.

From the trend lines in Figures 10, 11, and 12 it appears that the semi-log trend gives a better fit in the cases of transportation and manufacturing while the linear trend apparently gives a better fit for petroleum, agriculture, mining, and construction. The sum of these gives what is probably a more accurate projection of total consumption:

Petroleum	341,435
Agriculture	25,196
Mining	9,196
Construction	804,513
Transportation	213,727
Manufacturing	2,122,054
Total (metric tons of steel ingots)	3,516,121

The large difference between the linear projections and the log projections points up the major difficulty in making projections. It is

TABLE 33

Mexican Steel Consumption by Industrial Sectors
(Metric Tons of Steel Ingots)

Year	Agriculture	Construction	Transportation	Petroleum	Mining	Manufacturing
1953	3,515	210,872	174,848	129,159	5,272	354,968
1954	3,611	248,264	58,681	169,722	4,514	417,987
1955	2,215	266,923	182,748	172,780	6,645	476,252
1956	4,445	339,289	250,392	200,017	7,408	680,060
1957	10,015	430,626	307,112	272,062	8,345	640,931
1958	13,917	406,676	227,062	281,426	7,731	609,240
1959	13,489	433,134	65,944	269,772	5,995	710,399
1960	14,905	480,676	255,243	268,284	7,452	836,525
1961	14,179	515,761	155,969	242,815	7,090	836,561
1962	8,700	476,750	161,817	175,737	6,960	910,003
Total	88,991	3,808,971	1,839,826	2,181,774	66,412	6,472,926

Source: Salcido M., *El Mercado del Acero en México*, p. 45.

FIGURE 10

Trends for Steel Consumption by Transportation, Construction, and Manufacturing Sectors

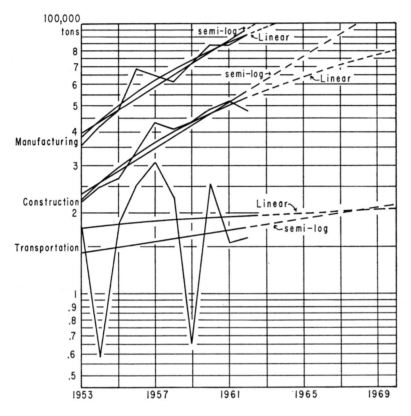

a matter of judgment as to whether the trend for construction consumption of steel (Figure 10) is linear or log. It appears, in the judgment of this writer, that the semi-log trend fits a little high and that the projection from that trend would be high. The shape of the construction trend is very similar to that of manufacturing except that construction has a slight downward trend for the last four years. It is probably for this reason that the linear trend appears to fit construction while the semilog trend fits manufacturing.

In Figure 14 semi-log trend lines have been fitted to aggregate data for steel consumption and production for the period 1953–

FIGURE 11

Trend for Petroleum Steel Consumption

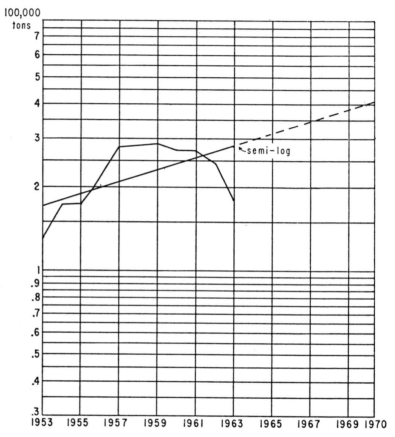

1963. One additional year has been included as compared to the preceding trends for sectoral consumption. Consumption by sector for the year 1963 was not available. It appears that the trend line for production is appropriately a semi-log trend, which indicates a constant rate of growth. With the consumption data the matter is not so obvious, as the slope of the plotted trend for the last three years indicates that a declining rate of growth may have set in. Obviously, three observations are not enough to constitute a trend; however, they should not be completely ignored. A linear trend line has therefore been plotted in addition to the log trend.

FIGURE 12

Trend for Mining Steel Consumption

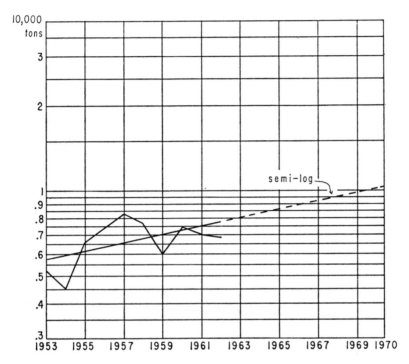

TABLE 34

Equations for Linear Projections

Sector	Equation[a]	1970 Projection
Petroleum	$Y = 173,804.62 + 9,860.62X$	341,435
Agriculture	$Y = 3,032.06 + 1,303.79X$	25,196
Mining	$Y = 5,857.40 + 196.40X$	9,196
Construction	$Y = 228,395.27 + 33,889.27X$	804,513
Transportation	$Y = 175,995.66 + 1,774.65X$	206,164
Manufacturing	$Y = 380,401.07 + 59,309.27X$	1,388.658
Total (metric tons of steel ingots)		2,775,162

[a] Where $Y =$ steel consumption and $X =$ years 1953–1962.

FIGURE 13

Trends for Agricultural Steel Consumption

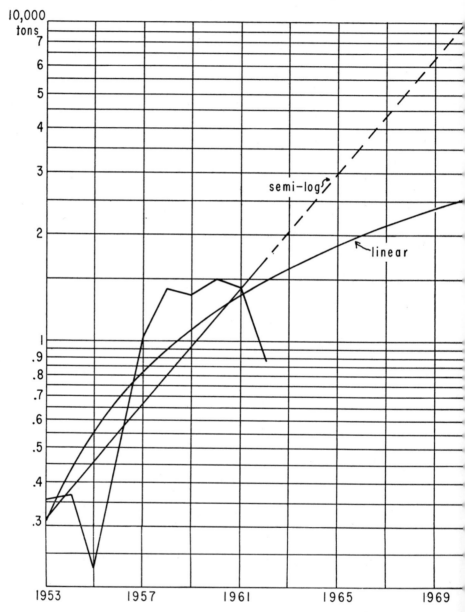

FIGURE 14

Trends for Production and Consumption of Steel

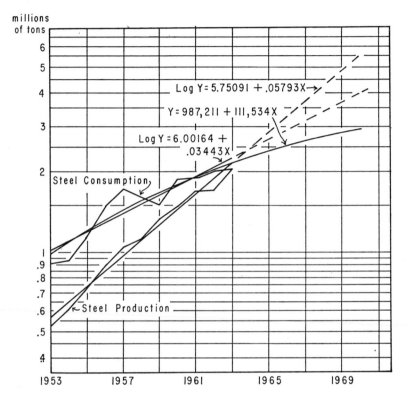

TABLE 35

Equations for Semi-Log Trend Projections

Sector	Equation[a]	1970 Projection
Petroleum	Log Y = 5.22571 + .02214X	399,960
Agriculture	Log Y = 3.49729 + .08139X	76,020
Mining	Log Y = 3.75675 + .01453X	10,089
Construction	Log Y = 5.37242 + .04231X	1,235,294
Transportation	Log Y = 5.17273 + .00924X	213,727
Manufacturing	Log Y = 5.60068 + .04270X	2,122,054
Total metric tons of steel ingots		4,057,144

[a] Where Y = steel consumption and X = years 1953–1962.

FIGURE 15

Trends for Consumption of Sheet, Plate, and Tinplate

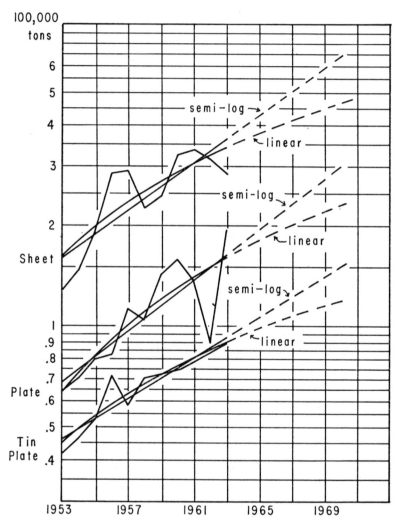

It appears that the best fit may be somewhere between the semi-log trend and the linear trend line, to indicate a somewhat declining rate of growth, but a rate faster than a fixed annual physical incre-

FIGURE 16

Trends for Consumption of Pipe and Wire

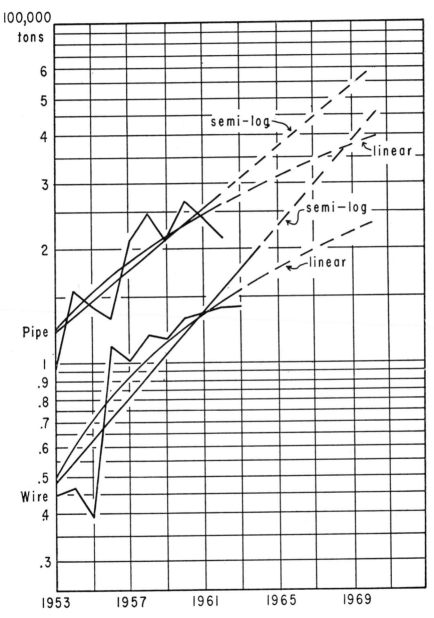

FIGURE 17

Trends for Consumption of Commercial Shapes

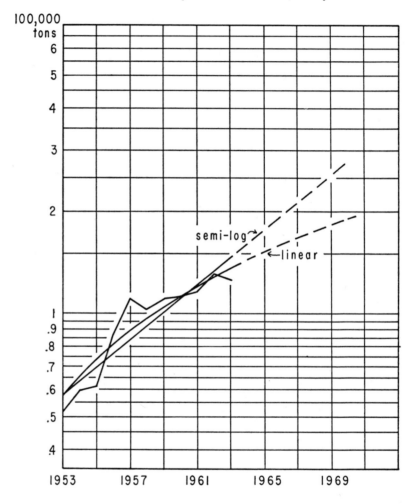

ment. Again the dilemma is pointed up in fitting trend lines from which to make projections. In the final analysis, judgment is required as to which trend line fits the data and hence which projection is to be accepted.

As regards production, it is obvious that the rate of growth of production is quickly approaching a ceiling to be placed on it by size of market outlet. In the past the new markets were found in Mexico, but in the future, exports will have to grow at a high rate if production is to keep up its established pace for more than a couple of years. For this reason no projections have been made from production data. Projections from aggregate consumption data for the year 1970 are, where Y = aggregate steel consumption and X = years 1953–1963: Linear trend: 2,883,297 tons ($Y = 1,097,211.6 + 111,534.5X$); and

Log trend: 3,863,245 tons ($\text{Log } Y = 6.00164 + .03443X$).

As mentioned previously, neither equation seems to give a perfect fit and it would probably be appropriate to select some point between the two projections. As a starting point the difference between the two might be split, to arrive at a projection of 3,373,271 tons of steel ingots. This method is admittedly a rough calculation and it would appear that a more scientific projection could be made by fitting trend lines to data that have been broken down on a product basis. The individual predictions could then be added to arrive at a total. The equations for the trend lines are presented in Tables 36 and 37.

For each of the flat-rolled products, a log-trend projection makes the better fit. This judgment is re-enforced by the apparent fit of the

TABLE 36

Semi-Log Trend Equations for Steel Products
(Metric Tons)

Product	Equation[a]
Tinplate	$\text{Log } Y = 4.66675 + .03015X$
Wire	$\text{Log } Y = 4.68770 + .05617X$
Com. Shapes	$\text{Log } Y = 4.77029 + .03973X$
Railway Steel	$\text{Log } Y = 4.96655 - .00656X$
Structural Shapes	$\text{Log } Y = 4.70388 + .01462X$
Plate	$\text{Log } Y = 4.83552 + .03809X$
Sheet	$\text{Log } Y = 5.20822 + .03545$
Construction Rods	$\text{Log } Y = 4.99168 + .05086$
Pipe[b]	$\text{Log } Y = 5.08234 + .04024$

Source: Equations have been fitted to consumption data in Chapter 5.
[a] Where Y = steel consumption and X = years 1953–1963.
[b] Data for seamless pipe, pipe with seam, and foundry pipe have been aggregated.

TABLE 37

Linear Equations for Steel Products
(Metric Tons)

Product	Equation[a]
Tinplate	$Y = 45,354.6 + 4414.9X$
Wire	$Y = 48,322.3 + 10805.6X$
Commercial Shapes	$Y = 57,688.2 + 7948.9X$
Railway Steel	$Y = 115,789.4 - 2740.7X$
Structural Shapes	$Y = 50,108.2 + 2148.2$
Plate	$Y = 63,346.8 + 9846.4X$
Sheet	$Y = 164,757.0 + 17873.9X$
Construction Rods	$Y = 69,761.9 + 20,180X$
Pipe[b]	$Y = 120,992.6 + 15838.6X$

Sources: Equations have been fitted to consumption data in Chapter 5.
[a] Where Y = steel consumption and X = years 1953–1963.
[b] 1953–62.

semi-log trend to the data for consumption of steel by the manufacturing sector. In selecting the semi-log trend, the assumption is
made that consumption of flat-rolled products will grow at a constant rate. One market for flat-rolled products which should help to
sustain the rate of growth is the automobile industry. Mexico is following an aggressive policy of import substitution of domestically
produced autos for imports. Present plans call for a limited number
of companies to manufacture autos in Mexico, utilizing 60–70 per
cent of the parts of domestic origin.[1] One estimate shows the Mexican auto industry consuming 115,500 tons of steel in 1970 as compared to 20,467 tons in 1962.[2] Not all of this will be flat-rolled
products, but the body and parts of the frame will utilize sheet and
plate.

The linear trend is assigned to building rods, commercial shapes,
and structural shapes. This choice would appear to be substantiated
by the use of a linear trend for the consumption of steel by the construction industry. For structural shapes and railway steel, the difference between the linear and semi-log trends is so slight that only
the semi-log trend is shown in Figures 18 and 19.

[1] Dale B. Truett, *The Development of the Transport Equipment Industry in Mexico*, p. 19.
[2] Nacional Financiera, S.A., *El Mercado de Valores*, XXIII, No. 22, pp. 299–301.

FIGURE 18

Trends for Consumption of Construction Rods and Structural Shapes

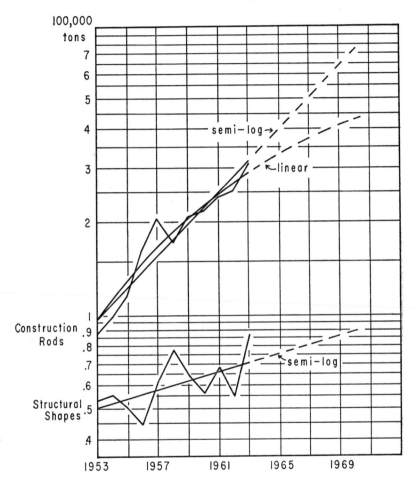

As previously pointed out, the petroleum industry has been an important consumer of pipe. The trend for consumption of steel by the petroleum industry takes a downward turn during the last few years and this fact re-enforces the choice of a linear trend rather than a log trend for pipe consumption.

The trend for wire consumption (Figure 16) appears to follow

FIGURE 19

Trend for Consumption of Railway Materials

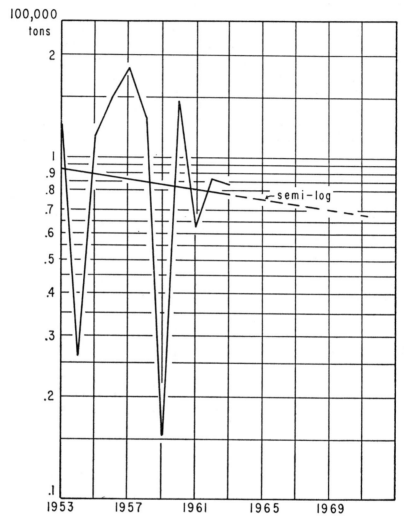

better the linear rather than the semi-log trend line. The large jump in consumption for the year 1956 distorts the trend which tapers off for the succeeding seven observations.

The projection for railway steel is made from the semi-log trend.

TABLE 38

Projections of Steel Demand for Mexico for the Year 1970

Product	Equation	Projection (metric tons)
Plate	Log Y = 4.83552 + .03809X	304,078
Sheet	Log Y = 5.20822 + .03545X	646,836
Tinplate	Log Y = 4.66675 + .03015X	151,122
Railway Steel	Log Y = 4.96655 + .00656X	69,493
Construction Rods	Y = 69.761.9 + 20,180.4X	430,991
Structural Shapes	Y = 50,108.2 + 2,148.2X	86,627
Commercial Shapes	Y = 57,688.2 + 7,948.9X	192,819
Pipe	Y = 120,992.6 + 15,838.6X	390,248
Wire	Y = 48,332.3 + 10,805.6X	232,017
Total		2,504,231

There is very little difference in the log projection and the linear projection (less than 500 tons) and to plot the linear trend in Figure 19 would result in an overlap and possible distortion of both trend lines.

The resulting projections, together with their equations, are presented in Table 38.

The above total is a projected consumption of finished steel for the year 1970. Often steel production and consumption figures are given in ingot equivalents, that is, the tonnage of steel ingots required to make the finished products. The ingot equivalent can be obtained by multiplying the above total by 1.333, which is the accepted conversion coefficient.[3] The resulting figure is 3,338,140 metric tons, which represent projected consumption of steel in ingot equivalents for the year 1970, based upon a summation of projections for individual steel products.

Projections of steel consumption for the year 1970 have been obtained, using three techniques: projection of aggregate consumption data, projection of consumption broken down by sectors, and on the basis of a breakdown by individual steel products. These projections are:

Aggregate projection ....3,373,271 tons (ingots)
Sectoral projection ....3,516,121 tons (ingots)
Product projection ....3,338,140 tons (ingots)

[3] Ralph J. Watkins, *The Market for Steel in Mexico*, p. 87.

While all three projections are close, that based on aggregates and that based on product breakdown are very close. The sectoral projection is higher, partly due to the fact that data for 1963 were not available on a sectoral basis. Aggregate consumption showed very little growth for 1963 over 1962. It will be recalled that the aggregate projection was arrived at by halving the difference between the semi-log and the linear projections, never a very scientific process. However, this judgment seems vindicated in light of the results of the projection on a product basis. It would seem that the projection on basis of product breakdown is likely to be more accurate than that based on aggregates, because individual fits can be made on a product basis and the various projections added. A projection for 1970 consumption of 3,338,000 tons of steel ingots is obtained in this manner.

7. Raw Materials and Fuels:
The Backward Linkages
of the Iron and Steel Industry

The inputs used by the steel industry constitute what Hirschman refers to as "backward linkage."[1] Accordingly, the establishment of an iron and steel industry should provide incentive for the establishment of domestic industries to supply steel's basic inputs. Hirschman speaks of backward linkage in terms of the creation of new firms; however, the definition can be carried further to include the inducement effect of additions to existing steel capacity upon the level of production of the suppliers of raw materials. Whether or not a domestic steel industry can exert a backward-linkage pull depends, of course, upon the existence of sufficient reserves of raw materials and fuels in the country in question.

The steel-making process requires many raw materials and fuels, including iron ore, coke, scrap iron and steel, limestone, ferroalloys, petroleum, and natural gas. The principal items of this group are ore, coke, scrap, and limestone, although all are important to the process. Figure 20 contains a simplified flow chart showing the approximate proportions in which these materials are combined in the Mexican steel industry.

The significance of Figure 20 is that it shows that there must be 1.6 tons of ore, 0.8 tons of coke, and 0.4 tons of limestone going into the blast furnace to obtain one ton of pig iron. Further, to obtain one ton of finished or intermediate steel, one ton of pig iron combines with 0.7 tons of scrap to produce 1.4 tons of steel in ingot form. The ingot is then rolled, with a loss that returns to the steel-making ovens as "home scrap" amounting to 0.4 tons for every 1.4 tons rolled.

In an integrated steel firm these three steps are all performed

[1] Hirschman, *Strategy of Economic Development*, pp. 98–119.

FIGURE 20

Input Coefficients for the Mexican Steel Industry

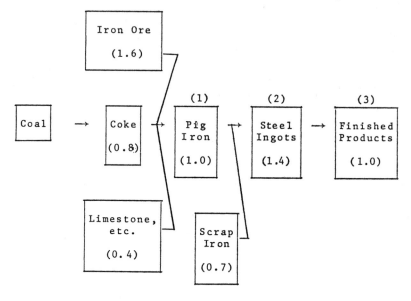

Source: Derived from tables in Comité para la Programación de la Industria Siderúrgica, *Programación del De-sarrollo de la Industria Siderúrgica Mexicana.*

by the same company. This is the case with Mexico's big three: AHMSA, Fundidora, and HYLSA. However, Mexico has some mills that perform only the third step, the fabrication of finished products. These companies purchase steel ingots, blooms, slabs, billets, or some other form of semifinished steel for their raw material input. In some areas, notably Japan, the second and third steps are commonly performed by one mill, with pig iron being the basic input purchased from outside the company. But for the integrated steel industry the backward-linkage effect of the production of finished steel works its "pull effect" only upon the basic raw materials— iron ore, coal, scrap, and fluxing materials—and not upon pig iron and steel-ingot production. Of course, a backward-linkage pull by the nonintegrated rolling mills is exerted upon the integrated mills which produce the pig iron and semifinished steel.

It goes without saying that there must be some provision for inputs for any steel industry, but these do not have to be of domestic origin. Fabricating mills are sometimes set up to use imported scrap, as was the case with HYLSA prior to the establishment of its sponge-iron producing subsidiary, Fierro Esponja, S.A. Since the supply of scrap is usually very small in undeveloped countries, the establishment of such fabricating mills is unlikely to call forth the necessary raw materials except through imports.

Just as the role of backward linkage is obvious, its impact is easily measured. The amount of domestically produced inputs used by the steel industry constitutes the backward-linkage effect of that industry. However, any volume of production of these inputs merely diverted from exports to domestic use would have to be subtracted from the total used by the domestic steel industry to arrive at the level of input production derived from the linkage pull of the new steel industry.

An illustration of the measurement of the backward-linkage effect can be derived from data on iron ore consumption in Mexico. The Mexican iron and steel industry consumed 1,583,814 tons of iron ore in 1961, and it has been projected that by 1967 annual consumption will be 4,574,000 tons,[2] or 2,991,000 more tons of iron ore than in 1961. The additional demand for iron ore would be the result of increased production of iron and steel, and 2,991,000 tons of ore measures the pull effect on the iron-ore-producing industries of that increment to production.

Yet this direct linkage effect cannot be said to be the extent of the impact of steel production upon iron-ore production. The increased domestic demand for iron ore may lead to economies of scale as the level of production increases and these economies may lead to lower price and more exports of ore. Conversely, increased exploitation of ore reserves might lead to diseconomies of scale due to a decreasing metal content of the ore, with concomitant increases in price and possible diminution of exports. Any such changes due to economies or diseconomies of scale should be charged or credited to indirect backward-linkage effects.

There follows a more comprehensive study of the industries that supply these basic inputs for the steel industry. The evaluation of linkage effects will be considered in connection with a general study of each industry in this general survey of the iron and steel industry.

[2] Comité para Programación de la Industria Siderúrgica, *Programación del Desarrollo de la Industria Siderúrgica Mexicana*, Tables 16 and 18.

Iron Ore

Iron ore is the basic raw material for an integrated steel industry. Many types of fluxes can be substituted for each other to be combined with the ore and several types of fuels can be used to reduce the ore to metal, but for the ore itself there is no substitute. An abundance of ore is found in Latin America, with a significant amount located in Mexico. Table 39 gives a breakdown of world iron ore reserves by area and Table 40 gives a breakdown of Latin American reserves by country.

It will be noted that Mexico ranks sixth in size of reserves of iron ore in Latin America and only fifth in actual mining of ore, as shown by the figures in Table 41. However, Mexico, unlike Venezuela, does not export significant amounts of ore.

Figures recently printed in *Comercio Exterior de México* show Mexico's ore reserves at approximately 570 million tons, broken down as follows:

Proven reserves ....244 million tons
Probable reserves .... 88 million tons
Possible reserves ....239 million tons[3]

These reserves are not concentrated in any particular area of the

TABLE 39

World Iron-Ore Reserves
(Millions of Tons)

Area	Ore Directly Utilizable	Mineral Utilizable after Benificiation
Canada	6,635	7,000
United States	4,500	60,400
Latin America	23,608	36,605
Western Europe	19,310	1,730
Eastern Europe	740	--------
U.S.S.R.	33,757	23,984
India	21,300	85,000
Japan	27	37

Source: Carlos Prieto, *Tres Industrias Mexicanas antes la ALAC*, p. 10.

[3] Banco Nacional de Comercio Exterior, S.A., *Comercio Exterior de México*, May, 1963 (English edition), p. 20.

TABLE 40

Iron-Ore Reserves in Latin America—Directly Utilizable
(Millions of Tons)

Country	Tons
Argentina	800
Bolivia	500
Brazil	16,250
Chile	190
Colombia	105
Cuba	3,000
Dominican Republic	43
Mexico	500[a]
Peru	740
Venezuela	2,200

Source: Carlos Prieto, *Tres Industrias Mexicana antes la ALAC*, p. 11.
[a] Latest estimates say 570 million tons (see Table 44).

country, but are located in many diverse areas. The map in Figure 21 shows the location of known iron ore deposits and Table 42 gives the magnitude of these ore reserves by geographic breakdown.

Only 23 per cent of these reserves, that portion located in the Northern Zone, are relatively close to accessible deposits of coking coal now being exploited in the state of Coahuila. The largest de-

TABLE 41

Production of Iron Ore in Latin America
(Thousand Metric Tons)

Country	1956	1957	1958	1959	1960	1961	1962
Argentina	33	32	29	48	58	60	....
Brazil	2,771	3,384	3,526	6,057	6,355	6,652	....
Chile	1,563	1,706	2,296	2,936	3,804	4,426	5,160
Colombia	168	253	238	172	178	268	270
Cuba	4	8	6	5	5	5	5
Mexico	489	569	581	535	521	687	1,091
Peru	1,614	2,148	1,544	2,092	2,818	3,057	3,247
Venezuela	7,107	9,024	9,136	10,149	13,474	9,322	8,490

Source: United Nations, *Statistical Yearbook, 1963*, pp. 175–176.

TABLE 42

Geographic Breakdown of Mexico's Iron-Ore Reserves
(Metric Tons)

Area	Tons
Northern Pacific Zone	63 million
States of Baja California	
Sinaloa	
Northern Zone	132 million
States of Chihuahua	
Coahuila	
Durango	
Tamaulipas	
Zacatecas	
Central Zone	37 million
States of Hidalgo	
México	
Morelos	
Puebla	
Veracruz	
Central Pacific Zone	281 million
States of Colima	
Guerro	
Jalisco	
Michoacán	
Southern Zone	57 million
States of Chiapas	
Oaxaca	
Total	570 million

Source: Cámara Nacional de la Industria del Hierro y del Acero, *Tercer Congreso Nacional de la Industria Siderúrgica, 1961*, p. 25.

posits of ore, those of the Central Pacific Zone, are not in the vicinity of coal deposits. Another problem of location is posed by the fact that the largest portion of the market for finished steel is located in the Federal District, yet the Central Zone has only 37 million tons of reserves. The ideal situation has both ore and coking coal located in the vicinity of the steel market.

Of the three largest steel plants in Mexico, two utilize ores from the Northern Zone. Altos Hornos obtains its ore from La Perla in Chihuahua, and La Fundidora mixes ores from Cerro de Mercado in Durango with ores obtained near Saltillo, Coahuila. The third, Hojalata y Lámina, S.A., obtains its ore at El Encino, Jalisco, on the Pacific coast. HYLSA located its plant in Monterrey at a great distance from the ore, but near the natural gas fields. This location fits the classic rule of thumb that calls for moving ore to fuel.

The Durango ore used by La Fundidora has a high phosphorus content and is mixed with ores of Saltillo to give a satisfactory ore with lower phosphorus content.[4] The result of the mixture is an ore with a lower metal content, as shown in Table 43.

An analysis of the ore of AHMSA's La Perla and HYLSA's El Encino is shown in Table 44.

All three, Cerro de Mercado, La Perla, and El Encino, use open-pit methods of mining, with explosives to break the ore loose and mechanical equipment, including bulldozers, to collect it.[5]

The discovery of presently used reserves in Mexico dates to 1552 when Cerro de Mercado was discovered. Prior to this century most iron ore was mined on a very small scale; however, with the establishment of Fundidora, Mexican iron-ore production found its first large outlet. Table 45 shows the production of ore from 1903 to 1963.

Iron-ore production grew at a rate of 9.8 per cent annually over

TABLE 43

Ores Used by La Fundidora

Mineral	Durango Ore (%)	Mixed Ore (%)
Iron (Fe)	60.30	49.01
Silicon Dioxide	3.98	5.77
Alumina	0.49	1.01
Calcium Oxide	1.95	5.11
Magnesium Oxide	0.29	0.37
Phosphorus	0.50	0.21
Manganese	0.06	0.99
Sulfur	0.158	0.063

Source: United Nations, *An Inquiry into the Iron and Steel Industry of Mexico*, p. 19.

[4] United Nations, *An Inquiry into the Iron and Steel Industry of Mexico*, pp. 18–19.

[5] Torón Villegas, *La Industria Siderúrgica*, pp. 160–161, 171, 175–176.

TABLE 44

Analysis of Ores at La Perla and El Encino

Mineral	El Encino (%)	La Perla (%)
Iron (Fe)	60.40	59.90
Phosphorus	0.32	0.55
Sulphur	0.13	0.11

Source: Carlos Prieto, "La Industria Siderúrgica," p. 226.

the period 1939–1960, and a projection of production data for that period indicates a production of approximately 1,684 tons for 1970. The projection was obtained by fitting the equation $\text{Log } Y = 1.9658 + .0407X$ to data for iron-ore production for 1939–1960.

It would appear that with reserves of 570 million tons of iron ore, Mexico has a reasonable base for an integrated industry. Assuming that the ore has a 60-per-cent iron content and that the steel furnace charge averages 70 per cent pig iron and 30 per cent scrap, the present reserves, if fully exploited, would support the production of close to 490 million tons of steel. However, as noted earlier, most of the reserves are located much further from the coal deposits than the reserves that are presently being exploited. Shifting from use of the northern reserves to any of the others might cause changes in the cost structure due to additional transportation costs or might lead to consideration of other locations for future capacity expansions.

Coal and Coke

Mexico does not import coal; therefore the amount of that mineral used to produce siderurgical coke is mined in Mexico and constitutes the technical linkage between the coal and steel industries.

Coal can be utilized by industries other than iron and steel and it is entirely possible that the coal industry, by virtue of achieving economies of scale due to increasing demand derived from the growth of steel production, would attract other industries to use coal as an input. Thus an interaction would be achieved between the backward linkage of steel and forward-linkage "push" effects of coal upon other industries. Such interaction, if extant, cannot be measured.

TABLE 45

Iron-Ore Production in Mexico
(Metric Tons)

Year	Production	Year	Production
1903	9,932	1934	133,421
1904	23,434	1935	116,260
1905	19,674	1936	146,783
1906	31,062	1937	158,421
1907	23,082	1938	125,733
1908	23,555	1939	154,050
1909	48,656	1940	132,014
1910	54,598	1941	94,619
1911	63,965	1942	106,529
1912	57,832	1943	147,059
1913	12,758	1944	134,632
1914	--------	1945	208,048
1915	1,714	1946	171,000
1916	19,981	1947	226,000
1917	19,119	1948	227,000
1918	25,891	1949	247,000
1919	30,904	1950	286,000
1920	26,034	1951	313,000
1921	34,110	1952	340,000
1922	41,574	1953	331,000
1923	50,694	1954	314,000
1924	52,448	1955	429,000
1925	127,492	1956	489,000
1926	92,982	1957	569,000
1927	64,000	1958	581,000
1928	80,293	1959	535,000
1929	112,749	1960	521,000
1930	106,979	1961	687,000
1931	65,156	1962	1,354,000
1932	27,122	1963	1,397,000
1933	77,714		

Source: For years 1903–1945, Jenaro González, *Riqueza Minera y Yacimientos Minerales de México,* p. 487; for years 1946–1960, United Nations, *Statistical Yearbook*; for years 1961–1963, Nacional Financiera, S.A., *Informe Anual, 1964.*

The thesis is often put forward that while there are many and large reserves of high-grade iron ore in Latin America, there is a

110 STEEL AND ECONOMIC GROWTH IN MEXICO

dearth of coking coal. This statement has validity when applied to most of the countries of Latin America. For example, Brazil and Venezuela have some of the world's largest iron-ore deposits yet Brazil has to resort to charcoal and asphalt in its fuel mix and Venezuela has no reserves of coking coal. However, Mexico stands as an exception to the rule, with reserves of 6.5 billion tons of coal.[6]

Although some of the major uses for coal, such as fuel for steam locomotives, have disappeared in recent decades, coal production in Mexico has grown at an annual rate of 3.4 per cent for the period 1939–1960. While coal production has been growing, coal consumption, as a proportion of all energy consumed, had fallen to 5.1 per cent in 1961 as compared with 11.2 per cent in 1940.[7] The growth of steel production, and especially of pig-iron production, has had a major impact on the coal industry. When coal production is correlated with pig-iron production for the period 1939 to 1960 the correlation coefficient is .87 (see Appendix C, No. 8). The dependence of coal production on the level of pig-iron production is a phenomenon of recent decades, as is revealed by a comparison of figures for total production of coal and iron ore for the period 1890 to 1946. Coal production during that period totaled 45,311,981 tons while iron-ore production was only 3,247,495 tons.[8] When it is considered that approximately 1.33 tons of coal are required to produce one ton of coke and that approximately 0.8 ton of coke is required in the production of one ton of pig iron, it is obvious from a historical comparison of the volumes of coal and pig-iron production that industries other than iron and steel were important consumers of coal. As previously mentioned, for many years railroads were an important outlet for coal production. De Silva divides Mexican coal exploitation into two periods with 1910 as the dividing line between the two.[9] Prior to 1910, railroads consumed most of Mexico's coal. At one time, almost all of the Sabinas basin was operated under concession by the Mexican National Railways.[10] De Silva's second period, dating from 1910 forward, was ushered in by the Revolu-

[6] Banco Nacional de Comercio Exterior, S.A., *Comercio Exterior de México*, May 1963 (English edition), p. 20.
[7] Freda Bullard, "Mexico's Natural Gas," p. 256.
[8] Jenaro González, *Riqueza Minera*, p. 448.
[9] José Antonio de Silva, "Problems of Utilizing Coal Resources in the Industrialization of Northern Mexico," *Basic Industries in Texas and Northern Mexico*, p. 65.
[10] *Ibid.*

tion, during which the National Railways of Mexico reduced their operations drastically and also began to convert to oil-burning locomotives.[11]

Mexico's coal industry is concentrated in the state of Coahuila where the names Rosita, Cloete, Aguita, Palaú, and Sauceda grace the mines that yield up this black fuel. The reserves at Sabinas in Coahuila are the oldest worked deposits of coal in Mexico. Sabinas Coal Mines, the first company of record in that region, was set up in 1884. The mine was called La Mina San Felipe. Although Sabinas Coal Mines was the first company of which there is a record, investigations indicate that there was mining in the region as far back as the early part of the nineteenth century.[12] It has been estimated that in all of Mexico approximately one million tons of coal had been mined prior to 1890.[13] Of this total, Sabinas Coal Mines accounted for a little more than 100,000 tons.[14]

The Coahuila Coal Company began work in the eight El Hondo mines in 1887, and between that date and the year 1904, when operations were closed down, 2.5 million tons of coal were mined and the company's 120 beehive ovens produced 350,000 tons of coke.[15]

In the year 1925, coal production reached its peak, with 1,444,498 tons being taken from the mines. Production then moved erratically downward until 1940 saw a production figure of only 815,907 tons; however, the trend was reversed in the 1940's and production began to increase, receiving a special boost from the expansion of steelmaking capacity during that decade. Table 46 gives coal production figures from the year 1891 through 1962.

As happened in Western Europe and the United States, early mining was with rather primitive and labor-intensive methods, put to work in unsafe mines. Imported Japanese labor was used in the first Coahuila mines,[16] a fact that De Silva attributes to the inability of the sparse population in Northern Mexico to supply the requisite labor.[17] Open flames were used in unventilated shafts and tunnels, with consequent heavy loss of life. Safety lamps were not intro-

---

[11] *Ibid.*
[12] Arnulfo Villarreal, *El Carbón Mineral en México*, p. 109.
[13] Jenaro González, *Riqueza Minera*, p. 394.
[14] *Ibid.*, p. 448.
[15] Villarreal, *El Carbón Mineral en México*, p. 109.
[16] De Silva, "Problems of Utilizing Coal Resources," p. 70.
[17] *Ibid.*

duced until the early 1920's.[18] Machine mining also was introduced in the early 1920's in the Rosita mines but in some small mining operations the pick and shovel still prevail.[19]

Reserves of both anthracite and bituminous coal are extensive in Mexico; however, only the bituminous coal can be used to make the coke necessary to feed the blast furnaces of the steel industry. Nevertheless, no shortage of coking coal is likely as the reserves in Coahuila alone are estimated to contain 2 billion tons of bituminous coking coal, with estimates for the country as a whole running as high as 6.5 billion tons.[20] The map in Figure 21 shows the locations of coal reserves.

Although bituminous coal is the type used for coking, some of its subclasses found in Mexico contain such a high degree of volatile material as to remove them from consideration as coking coal. A good coking coal should have a more or less solid mass and have a low content of both cinders and sulphur. Zimmermann says: "Coke is coal from which all ingredients other than carbon have been re-

FIGURE 21

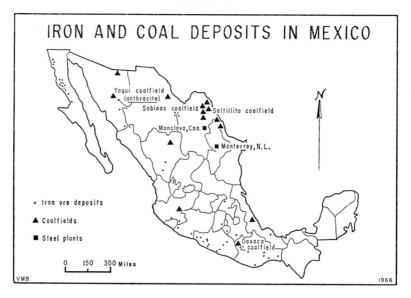

18 *Ibid.*
19 *Ibid.*
20 *Comercio Exterior de México*, May, 1963 (English edition), p. 20.

TABLE 46

Coal Production in Mexico
(Tons)

Year	Production	Year	Production
1521 } 1890	1,000,000	1926	1,226,808
		1927	1,031,308
1891	200,000	1928	1,022,475
1892	350,000	1929	1,059,956
1893	260,000	1930	1,071,658
1894	300,000	1931	922,289
1895	270,000	1932	690,805
1896	253,104	1933	646,838
1897	359,070	1934	782,156
1898	367,193	1935	1,255,058
1899	409,125	1936	1,307,915
1900	387,977	1937	1,242,148
1901	670,000	1938	1,093,252
1902	709,654	1939	876,851
1903	780,000	1940	815,907
1904	831,762	1941	855,697
1905	920,000	1942	914,269
1906	767,865	1943	1,025,326
1907	1,024,580	1944	904,198
1908	866,317	1945	914,614
1909	1,300,000	1946	983,000
1910	1,304,111	1947	1,040,000
1911	1,400,000	1948	1,057,000
1912	982,396	1949	1,075,000
1913	600,000	1950	912,000
1914	780,000	1951	1,104,000
1915	450,000	1952	1,317,000
1916	300,000	1953	1,432,000
1917	430,820	1954	1,314,000
1918	781,860	1955	1,342,000
1919	728,374	1956	1,408,000
1920	715,789	1957	1,421,000
1921	734,980	1958	1,471,000
1922	932,550	1959	1,586,000
1923	1,261,541	1960	1,772,000
1924	1,226,696	1961	1,068,006
1925	1,444,498	1962	1,103,793

Source: 1521–1945: Jenaro González, *Riqueza Minera*, p. 478; 1946–1960: United Nations, *Statistical Yearbook*; 1961–1962: Nacional Financiera, S.A., *Informe Anual, 1963.*

moved by combustion."[21] However, this is an oversimplification of the matter since coke has to have certain properties or qualities in order that it may be used in the blast furnace. Villareal says:

A good siderurgical coke must not contain more than 2 per cent of volatile material, 85 to 90 per cent of fixed carbon and 0.65 to 1.5 per cent of sulphur, but it is preferable that there be a lower content of sulphur to prevent its being passed into the iron.[22]

The phosphorus content should be low for the production of iron to be processed in open-hearth steel-making furnaces and very low (0.018 to 0.040 per cent) for the production of Bessemer steel. While the content of cinders can vary between 8 and 16 per cent, it is preferable that it not exceed 12 per cent and the moisture content should be less than 5 per cent.[23] A high content of cinders will result in the coke's being of a consistency that will not support the weight of the charge in the blast furnace.[24] Any sulphur transmitted to the pig iron will detract from the quality of the steel produced with that iron.

While anthracite coal is found in the states of Durango, Michoacán, Puebla, Sonora, and Tamaulipas, practically all of Mexico's coal production is of bituminous coal. And although bituminous coal is found in fourteen of Mexico's states, about 86 per cent of production comes from the Sabinas reserves and 13 per cent from Saltillo.[25]

The reserves in the Sabinas region are broken down by location in Table 47.

The coal is washed prior to use in the coking ovens to remove as much of the cinders as possible. Table 48 shows the composition of the coal in the Saltillo and Sabinas regions.

While coking coal in Mexico is plentiful, the reserves that are presently being mined are the ones of the north that are easily exploitable. A problem in the location of steel mills is posed by the presence of rich iron ore reserves in the south of Mexico, especially in the area known as Las Truchas. In order to employ these reserves in the blast furnace, either the coal would have to be transported to the location of the ore or the ore brought to the coal. For reasons discussed earlier, it is usually advisable to move ore to coal.

[21] Erich W. Zimmermann, *World Resources and Industries*, p. 491.
[22] Villarreal, *El Carbón Mineral en México*, p. 43.
[23] *Ibid.*
[24] *Ibid.*, pp. 27–28.
[25] *Ibid.*, p. 158.

TABLE 47

Coal Reserves of the Sabinas Region
(Thousands of Tons)

Location	Measured	Indicated	Inferred	Possible	Total
Las Adpuntas	954	2,809	37,400	510,710	551,873
Las Esperanzas	159	....	77,625	94,665	172,449
Monclova	....	....	....	5,616	5,616
Sabinas	125,650	40,210	397,010	714,570	1,277,440
Saltillo	35,192	42,282	9,634	576,328	663,636
San Patricio	2,809	20,600	....	1,300,591	1,324,000
San Salvador	94	281	468	....	843
Total	164,858	106,182	522,137	3,691,770	3,995,857

Source: Federico Pérez Molina, "La Industria Siderúrgica en la América Latina," p. 62.

Until 1924, all coke in Mexico was produced in old-fashioned beehive ovens. The first beehive ovens in the United States date to the early 1840's and they remained the only method of coking bituminous coal until the development of the Selmet-Solvay by-

TABLE 48

Analysis of Saltillo and Sabinas Coals

Mine	Volatile Material	Fixed Carbon	Ash	Sulphur
Saltillo				
Saltillito	21.6	51.9	26.5	------
Barroterán	22.5	49.4	28.1	------
Sabinas				
Rosita	24.4	47.1	28.5	1.10
Cloete	22.6	52.3	25.1	1.10
Palaú	21.2	57.2	21.6	1.30
Sauceda	21.1	55.4	22.5	1.30
Sabinas	22.0	52.6	25.4	------
San Felipe	19.2	60.9	19.9	1.25
El Coyote	20.8	54.1	25.1	1.25

Source: Salvador Cortés Obregón, "The Coal Used in the Mexican Iron and Steel Industry," in United Nations, *A Study of the Iron and Steel Industry in Latin America*, II, 43.

product ovens, the first of which was built in the United States in 1893.[26] This was followed in 1898 by the famous by-product oven of Heinrich Koppers of Germany.[27] By 1919, the production of coke in by-product ovens in the United States exceeded the production of the beehive ovens.[28] However, in Mexico, the first by-product ovens were not introduced until 1924 when the Compañía Carbonífera de Sabinas, S.A. introduced forty Wilputte Underjet by-product ovens into its plant at Nueva Rosita.[29] Later, in 1955, the Compañía Mexicana de Coque y Derivados, S.A., de C.V. ("Mexcoq" is the commonly used abbreviation for this company) was organized in Monclova as a subsidiary to AHMSA; this company has fifty-seven Koppers chamber ovens which are designed to recover by-products.[30] Although the combined capacity of these two is almost 700,000 tons of coke annually and more than sufficient to satisfy present demand, there exist in northern Mexico about seven hundred beehive ovens, most of which are closed down because they are not competitive with the by-product ovens; however, they could easily be reactivated if ever needed.[31]

In the United States, by-product coke ovens are generally found in conjunction with steel mills, with the coking ovens joined by pipe to the blast furnaces so that the heat required for the coking process can be obtained from the blast furnace. As of 1963, the ovens of Mexcoq were linked to the AHMSA blast furnaces. In addition to the savings in heat, the very name, by-product oven, gives a clue as to its primary advantage over the beehive oven. The gas produced in the coking process is a combination of tar, which is a condensable element, and of noncondensable elements, such as ammonia, benzene, and other combustible hydrocarbon gases.[32] The gases leave the coking ovens through vertical pipes where their temperature is dropped from 600 degrees centigrade to between 75 and 80 degrees centigrade. The tar is precipitated early and then one by one various other by-products are captured. The variety of by-products can be illustrated by itemizing the productive capacity

[26] Zimmermann, *World Resources and Industries*, p. 491.
[27] *Ibid.*
[28] *Ibid.*
[29] De Silva, "Problems of Utilizing Coal Resources," p. 65.
[30] Prieto, "La Industria Siderúrgica," p. 231.
[31] *Ibid.*
[32] Torón Villegas, *La Industria Siderúrgica*, pp. 16–17.

TABLE 49

By-Product Capacity of Mexicana de Coque
y Derivados, S.A. de C.V.

Coal Used	1,010,000
Coke Produced	710,000
Coke Gas Produced	164,125,000 m³/year
Ammonium Sulphate	7,500
Benzene	3,200
Toluene	950
Xilenos	500
Naphtha	1,200
Creosote	1,800
Tar	12,000

Source: Luis Torón Villegas, *La Industria Siderúrgica*, p. 20.

of Mexcoq, the company adjacent to the Monclova blast furnaces. This has been done in Table 49.

The by-product ovens used by Mexcoq are of the most modern type. They have a daily capacity for taking a 2,860-ton charge of coal and producing 2,150 tons of coke. Since the period required for coking is somewhere between fourteen and seventeen hours, the above daily figures are based on averages computed from a production series. The capacity of the plant when in full production (around-the-clock) is 710,000 tons annually.[33]

Until January, 1963, the gas used as a fuel for converting the coal to coke was derived from the gas recovered from the coking process itself. Approximately 45 per cent of the gas siphoned off from the coking ovens was returned to them as a combustant. However, beginning in 1963, gas from the blast furnaces was used to heat the coke ovens, thus releasing the coke gases for distillation of by-products.[34] Gas from Mexcoq is now sold to Fertilizantes de Monclova, S.A., for use in making fertilizers. This company's plant is located 2.5 kilometers from the coking ovens. The company is independent of AHMSA and is owned by Nacional Financiera, French stockholders, and domestic stockholders in approximately equal shares.[35]

[33] *Ibid.*, pp. 15–16.   [34] *Ibid.*, p. 16.   [35] *Ibid.*, p. 21.

The production of these by-products and the accompanying employment are ultimately derived from the fact of domestic steel production but this production is not comprehended within the framework of the linkage concept, as normally defined. However, it might properly be thought of as a secondary backward linkage of the iron and steel industry.

Scrap

A significant raw material in the steel-making process is scrap, both iron and steel. Scrap is the one basic raw material used in the production of steel that is presently in short supply in Mexico. A popular notion is that a steel industry uses scrap when there is a shortage of pig iron for the steel furnaces, such as has been the case with the Japanese steel industry. However, scrap is a necessary ingredient in the normal steel-making process, whether it be in Japan, Mexico, or the United States. In 1948, the steel production of the United States utilized 52 per cent pig iron and 48 per cent scrap while in Mexico the relationship is similar, with scrap and pig iron each accounting for about 50 per cent of the weight of the steel produced.[36] Although the ratio of scrap to pig iron can properly be much less than 50 to 50, some scrap must be present in the charge of the open-hearth furnace for the steel produced to have the desired quality.

The scrap used in the charge to the open-hearth furnace derives from two sources: (1) scrap produced within the steel mill ("home scrap"), and (2) old steel derived from used machinery, autos, etc. The home scrap is a considerable proportion of the total and is the wastage involved in reducing, cutting, and milling the ingot into finished steel products. In 1961, the Siemens-Martin furnaces of the Mexican steel industry consumed 300,471 tons of home scrap as compared to 163,908 tons of exogenous scrap.[37] A breakdown of scrap consumption by source for the year 1949 shows the relative importance of the three sources of scrap for that year. This breakdown was:

Home scrap ....112,192 tons
Purchases on Mexican market ....152,168 tons
Imports (approximate) ....100,000 tons[38]

[36] Joaquín de la Peña, *La Industria Siderúrgica en México*, p. 31.
[37] Comité para Programación, *Programación de la Industria Siderúrgica*, Table 17.
[38] Peña, *La Industria Siderúrgica*, p. 95.

Due to the scarcity of domestic scrap, Mexico must import a large percentage of her requirements. Such shortage is natural in those nations with underdeveloped economies. The principal sources of scrap in developed economies are: old ships, railroad material, old machinery, junk automobiles, armaments, domestic utensils, etc. Mexico does not have caches of old armaments; old autos find ready markets and remain in use much longer than in the United States; and machinery determined obsolete by the larger manufacturer is often sold to smaller companies for further use. Therefore, Mexico does not produce its own requirements of scrap as do those countries with more highly developed economies. The principal domestic sources for scrap are Ferrocarriles Nacionales and Petroleos Mexicanos, these two furnishing more scrap than all other sources combined. However almost all of the scrap imports come from the United States.[39]

No time series of data was available as to the volume of domestic exogenous scrap utilized in Mexico. However, import figures are available and are presented in Table 50. It will be noted that these imports have increased steadily since 1944.

In addition to the scrap metal mixed into the charge of the open-hearth furnaces, some small operations reduce scrap in small electric furnaces for the production of steel, especially for the manufacture of specialty items.

To the extent that the scrap metal inputs of the steel industry derive from imports, no backward-linkage inducement effects are at work. Further, as the growth of steel production increases the demand for scrap imports, the foreign exchange loss due to such imports is increased. This loss is subsumed under the heading "Payments to Foreign Factors," in the discussion in Chapter 3. As regards that scrap obtained in Mexico, it would be a stretch of the linkage concept to hold that increased demand for scrap derived from steel production was tantamount to calling new productive forces into being. The scrap is not the result of new productive forces; rather it is a residue of rejected machines and artifacts of an industrial economy.

Other Raw Materials and Fuels

In addition to the major raw materials and fuels used in producing

[39] *Ibid.*, pp. 95, 100.

TABLE 50

Imports of Scrap Iron and Steel into Mexico
(Metric Tons)

Year	Tons	Year	Tons
1939	27,617	1952	132,340
1940	35,968	1953	142,023
1941	30,128	1954	206,861
1942	13,713	1955	236,435
1943	17,104	1956	290,672
1944	13,923	1957	288,884
1945	21,778	1958	259,817
1946	45,708	1959	389,365
1947	39,061	1960	374,137
1948	32,718	1961	354,520
1949	103,346	1962	281,765
1950	119,136	1963	456,850
1951	112,337		

Sources: Marcelo G. Aramburu, "El Crecimiento de la Industria Siderúrgica en México," Cámara Nacional del Hierro y del Acero, *Primero Congreso*, pp. 89–91; Cámara Nacional del Hierro y del Acero, *Circular No. 17*.

iron and steel, other materials play an important role in the technical process and also show linkage response to the "demand pull" of the steel industry. Three energy sources in addition to coal are prominent in the Mexican steel industry. These are natural gas, electricity, and petroleum. Raw materials used in addition to iron ore and scrap iron include limestone, fluorspar, graphite, and manganese.

In 1961, the Mexican steel industry consumed 5,783,000,000 kilowatt hours of electrical energy.[40] This consumption was not limited to the electric furnaces, although these furnaces did account for more than half of the total. A breakdown of this consumption is given in Table 51. An undetermined amount of this electricity is produced by generating facilities owned by the steel companies. "Consumption of natural gas in the large steel complexes includes utilization in fueling their private electric generating plants."[41]

[40] Comité para Programación, *Programación de la Industria Siderúrgica*, Table 17.
[41] Bullard, "Mexico's Natural Gas," p. 228.

TABLE 51

Consumption of Electrical Energy by the Mexican
Steel Industry by Process in 1961

Process	Kilowatt Hours Consumed (10^6 KWH)
Blast Furnaces	26.6
Sponge Iron	1.4
Open Hearth	20.9
Electric Furnaces	314.0
Rolling Mills	211.3
Other	4.0
Total	578.2

Source: Comité Para Programación, *Programación de la Industria Siderúrgcia*, Table 17.

AHMSA owns two power plants with a total of seven turbo-generators that have a combined capacity of 51,360 kilowats. These generators are powered by natural gas.[42] Fundidora also has two power plants, these having a total capacity of 60,000 kilowats.[43] Some of the Fundidora turbines burn natural gas and some utilize gas from the blast furnaces. Fundidora has a surplus of power, which it sells to the Federal Electricity Commission.

Obviously, the increase in steel production occasioned by the new investments since 1940 has been accompanied by increased demand for electrical energy. And to cite a specific example, the establishment of HYLSA in Monterrey exercised a definite backward-linkage pull through its giant electric furnaces. It is not determined whether this pull merely resulted in fuller use of existing electric power capacity or required the expansion of capacity.

Both natural gas and fuel oil are used as combustants in the iron- and steel-making processes. As previously described, HYLSA in Monterrey uses natural gas to reduce iron ore to a sponge iron that can be used as a substitute for pig iron or scrap in the electric steel-making furnaces. But as with electric power, the use of natural gas is not confined to special processes, but also finds significant usage in the standard processes, especially in the Siemens-Martin fur-

[42] Torón Villegas, *La Industria Siderúrgica*, pp. 45–46.
[43] *Ibid.*, pp. 90–92.

naces and the "soaking pits" located near the primary rolling mills. In 1961, the industry consumed 4,237,000,000 cubic meters of natural gas.[44] Of this, 484,000,000 cubic meters was consumed in the making of sponge iron, 591,000,000 cubic meters in the open-hearth furnaces, and the remainder, 3,162,000,000 cubic meters, apportioned to the fabrication of finished products. Also, as mentioned previously, natural gas is used to power turbo-electric generators owned by several of the steel companies.

Three companies pipe natural gas to Monterrey from the gas fields of Reynosa. These are La Compañía Mexicana de Gas, S.A., Gas Industrial de Monterrey, S.A., and Petróleos Mexicanos, S.A. Petróleos Mexicanos pipes gas from Monterrey to Monclova.[45] La Consolidada at Piedras Negras imports gas from Texas.[46] The latter's requirements would not constitute a backward-linkage pull. It has been estimated that industry in Monterrey accounts for 40 per cent of natural gas consumption in the North Zone; of this, Fundidora and HYLSA are mentioned as the major consumers.[47] The North Zone refers to the area beginning with Monterrey and moving north and west to encompass the states of Chihuahua, Coahuila, and Nuevo León. This gas is transmitted from the Reynosa fields. AHMSA is reported to account for 10 per cent of natural gas consumption in that zone. Here again, it is not possible to determine whether or not the gas consumption by the steel industry has resulted in added productive capacity for the natural gas producers.

The use of fuel oil is more limited, being used only as a combustant in the open-hearth furnaces. The oil is sprayed across the fiery bath in the hearth. Natural gas and fuel oil are sprayed from alternating nozzles and together furnish the heat necessary to refine the charge of pig iron and scrap into molton steel. In 1961, the industry consumed 513,000,000 liters of fuel oil in its Siemens-Martin furnaces.

Large quantities of limestone are used as fluxing material in the blast furnaces and open hearth furnaces. In 1961, the Mexican

[44] Comité para Programación, *Programación de la Industria Siderúrgica*, Table 17.

[45] Carlos Prieto, "La Industria Siderúrgica," pp. 231–232.

[46] United Nations, *An Inquiry into the Iron and Steel Industry of Mexico*, p. 11.

[47] Bullard, "Mexico's Natural Gas, p. 228.

industry consumed 455,659 tons of limestone.[48] Both AHMSA and Fundidora own large reserves of limestone that are located near their respective plants.[49]

Most of the ferroalloys used in steel making are produced in Mexico. AHMSA produces its own ferromanganese, Ferroaleaciones de México, an affiliate of Fundidora, supplies that company's needs.[50] The ferrosilica and silicamanganese used by the industry is produced by Tezintlan Copper Co., S.A., and Ferroaleaciones de México, S.A. Some ferroalloys, ferrocrome, ferromolybdenum, ferrotungsten, and ferrovanadium are not produced in Mexico and must be imported. In 1961, the industry consumed 288,014 tons of manganese and 31,356 tons of various other ferroalloys.[51]

An item of major importance to the iron and steel industry is refractory brick or "fire brick," which is used to line both the blast furnaces and open-hearth furnaces as well as the soaking pits. These bricks are of two types: acid brick and base brick. The acid is used in furnace linings when the charge contains impurities that are base and the base brick when the charge is acid. Both types of refractory brick are manufactured in Mexico; however, the magnesita and chrome for base bricks are imported.[52] The acid bricks, containing large quantities of silica, are manufactured by Harbison Walker Flir, S.A., in both Monterrey and Mexico City. Fundidora is an important participant in this company. Base refractory bricks are produced by General Refractories de México, S.A., in Ramos Arizpe, Coahuila.

Indirect Linkages

While no precise measure was given to the backward-linkage effects of the steel industry upon fuel and raw materials output, it is obvious that by virtue of utilizing a large proportion of domestically produced fuels, ores, and fluxes in its input mix, the pull effect has been strong. Ore, unlike coal, is utilized only by the iron and steel industry and its increased production is unlikely to have forward-linkage effects on industries other than steel. However, iron-ore

[48] Comité para Programación, *Programación de la Industria Siderúrgica*, Table 17.
[49] Torón Villegas, *La Industria Siderúrgica*, pp. 187–188.
[50] *Ibid.*, p. 49.
[51] Comité para Programación, *Programación de la Industria Siderúrgica*, Table 17.
[52] Torón Villegas, *La Industria Siderúrgica*, p. 190.

mining, as well as that of coal and fluxing materials, will have backward-linkage effects. These have been especially marked in the transportation industry. Table 52 shows the number of rail carloads of raw materials delivered to AHMSA during 1948 and 1954 respectively.

To the extent that the rail cars are produced domestically, as is now the case in Mexico, the additional rail cars required to haul these raw materials result from demand derived from the production of iron and steel. Since rail cars can be used over and over to haul these materials the data in Table 52 does not show the physical number of rail cars added to the Mexican economy as the result of the operations of AHMSA. However, the number of rail cars owned by steel companies and purchased from domestic manufacturers constitutes at least a part of the backward-linkage effect of the iron and steel industry upon the rail car industry. Both Fundidora and AHMSA own a considerable fleet of rail cars and the number of those cars produced in Mexico constitutes part of the backward-linkage effect of the steel industry upon the rail car industry. Any additions to the fleet of rail cars of the railroad companies due to increased hauling of raw materials for the steel companies would also be credited to the backward-linkage pull of the iron and steel industry. Forward linkage was also at work here. It cannot be

TABLE 52

Rail Carloads of Raw Materials and Fuels Received by
Altos Hornos de México, S.A. in 1948 and 1954

Raw Material	1948	1954
Iron Ore	2,083	5,112
Coal	899	1,133
Coke	2,787	6,734
Scrap	448	1,125
Refractory Brick	245	561
Petroleum	2,052	2,596
Limestone	28	234
Manganese	67	306
Total	8,609	17,801

Source: Cámara Nacional de la Industria del Hierro y del Acero, *Primer Congreso*, p. 20.

doubted that the availability of domestically produced steel plate played a major role in the decision of the government to establish Constructura Nacional de Carros de Ferrocarril, S.A., a company established for the construction of rail cars. The linkages concept becomes complicated and circular, but in this case it is easy to pinpoint that place in the circle where the action was initiated. It was with the iron and steel industry. The forward-linkage push of available domestic rail cars to haul new materials would not be a significant factor in causing a potential decision to become a decision-infact to build a domestic steel industry. Nor would the backward-linkage pull effects of a rail car industry have sufficient demand to cause the establishment of a steel industry. The steel industry created a demand for rail cars and produced the principal input for rail car production.

It is easy to conceptualize a continuous series of secondary, tertiary, etc. linkages, many of which, as in the case of rail cars, come full circle to exercise backward-linkage effects on the steel industry.

In the case of coal, another type of secondary backward linkage can be observed, in the coke by-product industries, particularly those connected with AHMSA, where the gas derived from coke is used in the production of chemicals. This secondary backward linkage of the steel industry is, of course, a forward linkage of the coal and coke industries for those industries using the chemicals, such as Fertilizantes de Monclova, S.A. Although ultimately resulting from backward-linkage effects of steel production upon coke production, this represents forward-linkage effects of coke production.

These diverse effects of a steel mill upon the economy in general and its immediate geographical location in particular can be put in better perspective by listing the subsidiary operations of AHMSA. This listing is shown in Table 53.

In making the decision to install a steel mill, planners in an underdeveloped economy can plan upon production and employment to have much greater impact than might be imagined from viewing data limited to the plant, stock of machinery and equipment, and size of work force for the steel mill itself. However, it is entirely possible that the planners could not, or would not, want to rely upon other decision-making units to succumb to the backward-linkage pull, and provide the necessary inputs of raw materials, fuel, and transportation facilities. In such a case, the decision to invest in a

TABLE 53

Subsidiary Operations of AHMSA
(in thousands of pesos of stock owned by AHMSA)

Firm	Activity	Capital Stock	Partici-pation of AHMSA
Cía. Mex. de Coque y Derivados, S.A.	Production of coke	$70,000.0	88.5%
La Perla, Minas de Fierro, S.A.	Iron ore mining	40,000.0	70.0
Guadalupe	Administrative company with manganese reserves	12,000.0	70.0
Eléctrica Monclova	Distribution of electric energy	1,700.0	58.8
Servicios Sociales Industriales, A.C.	Social services	273.1	81.0
Altos Hornos Comercial, S.A.	Product distribution	5,000.0	80.0
Laminadora Nacional, S.A.	Production of corrugated sheet	40,000.0	99.3
Florida de Muzquiz, S.A.	Coal mining	1,000.0	70.0
Mimosa	Coal mining	700.0	31.0
Barblock, S.A.	Production of barbed wire	2,630.0	99.8
Cía. Mex. de Tubos, S.A.	Production of pipe	n.d.	n.d.
Hotel Chulavista		n.d.	n.d.

Source: Agustín Acosta Lagunos, "Consideraciones sobre el Análisis Económico de Empresas."

steel mill would require concomitant decisions to provide for these items. The investment in a given size of steel mill might require considerably more funds in an underdeveloped country than in the United States. Further, it should be remembered that where domestic reserves of any raw material or fuel are inadequate, the backward-linkage pull will express itself through increased imports.

8. Mexican Foreign Trade in Iron and Steel Products

Prior to implementation of an import substitution policy a considerable proportion of Mexico's steel consumption derived from imports. For the period 1943–1947, imports averaged 51.4 per cent of steel consumed, but by the years 1959–1963 this percentage had dropped to 10.7. Not only did imports as a percentage of consumption decline, but the physical volume of imports also declined. For the years 1954–1958 the average annual volume of imports was 260,794 tons while during the succeeding five-year period (1959–1963), the annual average was 148,134 tons. This diminution in imports occurred in spite of the fact that steel consumption more than doubled between 1954 and 1963. Data for consumption and imports of steel are presented in Table 54.

Excluded from the import figures in Table 54 is the volume of imports of scrap iron and steel. The importation of scrap is a necessary although unhappy corollary to domestic steel production in Mexico because Mexico, like most countries newly embarked on the road to industrialization, has a dearth of scrap metal. The relative proportion of scrap to total imports can be discerned from Tables 55 and 56. Table 55 presents physical volume of imports on a product basis and Table 56 gives the percentage of the total for each product for each of the years 1953 through 1963.

It will be noted from Table 56 that finished steel as a percentage of total steel imports has been declining. Further, the physical volume of finished product imports has declined over the period 1953–1963. Among the finished products, rails and maintenance of way material have been, with the exception of two years, consistently a large proportion of imports. As was pointed out in Chapter 5, rails and maintenance of way material have not been the object

TABLE 54

Consumption and Imports of Steel
(Thousands of Metric Tons)

Year	Consumption[a]	Imports[b]	Imports/Consumption (%)
1942	224,348	67,426	30.1
1943	267,590	110,019	41.1
1944	401,903	217,404	40.2
1945	435,217	224,461	35.2
1946	510,143	261,929	51.3
1947	562,084	305,874	54.4
1948	433,080	168,256	38.9
1949	490,533	162,803	33.2
1950	591,084	246,510	41.7
1951	802,592	390,083	48.6
1952	759,001	314,504	41.4
1953	679,373	253,979	37.4
1954	697,520	194,410	27.9
1955	854,307	237,643	27.8
1956	1,117,957	333,037	29.8
1957	1,285,359	307,726	23.9
1958	1,216,683	231,153	19.0
1959	1,139,304	73,118	6.4
1960	1,396,499	221,117	15.8
1961	1,424,004	137,633	9.7
1962	1,424,675	150,634	10.6
1963	1,516,237	158,170	10.4

Sources: Consumption: Table 16, Chapter 5; Imports: 1942–1951, United Nations, *A Study of the Iron and Steel Industry in Latin America*, p. 443; 1952, Cámara Nacional de la Industria del Hierro y del Acero, *Primer Congreso*, pp. 85–91; 1952–1963, Cámara Nacional de la Industria del Hierro y del Acero, *Circular No. 17*, September 14, 1964.

[a] The consumption data have been converted from ingots to finished-product equivalent by applying the coefficient 17501.

[b] These data exclude imports of scrap, ferroalloys, and other primary materials.

of an import substitution policy, whereas steel plate, tin plate, and pipes have been. Steel companies with a capacity to produce rails and maintenance material have preferred to use that capacity to make structural shapes which command a higher profit. Also, the financing of purchases is a major consideration on the part of the

TABLE 55

Imports of Steel Products into Mexico
(Metric Tons)

Products	1953	1954	1955	1956	1957	1958	1959	1960	1961	1962	1963
Primary Material	148,932	238,735	290,109	395,727	448,954	400,601	446,708	402,735	374,413	290,702	458,883
1. Scrap	142,023	206,861	236,435	290,672	288,884	259,817	389,365	374,137	354,726	281,675	456,850
2. Laminating Material	2,583	3,232	6,309	50,563	34,226	46,831	13,259	24,021	17,543	7,462	————
3. Pig Iron	1,525	350	215	28	29	27	2	1	436	10	42
4. Steel Ingots	1,457	26,841	44,175	51,602	122,256	28,829	40,258	2,508	14	21	8
5. Alloys	1,344	1,451	2,975	2,862	3,559	5,097	3,824	2,048	1,694	1,534	1,983
Finished Steel Products	253,979	194,410	237,643	333,037	307,726	231,153	73,118	221,117	137,633	150,634	158,170
1. Plate	5,822	6,087	6,353	5,516	6,419	5,063	4,588	4,376	5,029	2,845	2,204
2. Sheet	21,937	13,832	12,202	58,019	18,601	9,782	7,655	15,894	14,062	12,117	13,986
3. Tinplate	16,208	10,262	20,111	29,335	16,614	3,183	1,039	2,444	2,243	4,854	7,228
4. Strip	5,489	6,922	8,891	13,255	8,293	7,447	3,203	1,361	1,600	943	1,408
5. Rods for Concrete	4,413	3,764	5,383	3,443	3,888	2,205	794	69	12	59	46
6. Other Rods	2,900	10,311	7,729	9,240	13,020	8,628	13,346	11,239	12,764	12,426	10,347
7. Wire	18,021	16,684	5,035	23,105	9,789	11,802	7,559	10,116	6,125	2,902	2,857
8. Cable	2,327	2,614	3,331	3,348	2,867	2,135	1,082	1,135	461	1,013	2,969

9. Rails and Maintenance of Way	100,975	5,902	95,922	118,376	161,683	121,320	1,322	123,917	50,511	77,405	60,985
10. Pipe	46,039	88,795	51,020	40,917	33,011	25,356	7,674	19,096	17,788	13,094	17,945
11. Pipe Connections	1,491	514	791	1,093	1,899	2,566	1,121	4,153	2,970	2,856	2,655
12. Drainage Pipe	2	--------	1	48	184	234	36	66	24	85	51
13. Structural Shapes	16,161	11,221	5,868	7,108	12,224	10,225	6,345	9,421	8,216	5,505	23,769
14. Spikes and Nails	195	229	298	348	1,322	609	830	1,436	1,003	899	1,045
15. Screws and Rivets	1,631	1,226	2,128	1,361	976	962	513	669	661	610	493
16. Chain	657	642	768	844	879	1,252	255	380	253	237	692
17. Iron and Steel Containers	3,075	3,489	2,612	4,396	6,537	3,848	3,339	3,936	3,989	4,354	2,672
18. Tin Cans	6,636	11,916	9,200	13,285	9,520	14,536	12,417	11,429	9,922	8,506	5,953
Total	402,911	433,145	527,752	728,764	756,680	631,754	519,826	623,852	512,047	441,336	617,053

Source: Cámara Nacional de la Industria del Hierro y del Acero, *Circular No. 17*.

TABLE 56

Breakdown of Imports of Steel Products as a Percentage of Total Steel Imports

Products	1953 %	1954 %	1955 %	1956 %	1957 %	1958 %	1959 %	1960 %	1961 %	1962 %	1963 %
Total	100.0	100.0	100.0	100.0	100.0	100.0	100.0	100.0	100.0	100.0	100.0
Primary Material	37.0	55.1	55.0	54.3	59.3	63.4	85.9	64.6	73.1	65.9	74.4
1. Scrap	35.2	47.8	44.8	40.0	38.2	41.1	74.9	60.0	69.3	63.8	74.0
2. Laminating Material	0.6	0.7	1.2	6.9	4.5	7.4	2.6	3.9	3.4	1.7	---
3. Pig Iron	0.4	---	---	---	---	---	---	---	---	---	---
4. Steel Ingots	0.3	6.2	8.4	7.1	16.2	4.6	7.7	0.4	---	---	---
5. Alloys	0.3	0.3	0.3	0.4	0.5	0.8	0.7	0.3	0.3	0.3	0.4
Finished Steel Products	63.0	44.9	45.0	45.7	40.7	36.6	14.1	35.4	26.9	34.1	25.6
1. Plate	1.4	1.4	1.2	0.8	0.8	0.8	0.9	0.7	1.0	0.6	0.4
2. Sheet	5.4	3.1	2.3	8.0	2.5	1.5	1.5	2.5	2.7	2.7	2.3
3. Tinplate	4.0	2.4	3.8	4.0	2.2	0.5	0.2	0.4	0.4	1.1	1.2
4. Strip	1.4	1.6	1.7	1.8	1.1	1.2	0.6	0.2	0.3	0.2	0.2
5. Rods for Concrete	1.1	0.9	1.0	0.5	0.5	0.3	0.1	---	---	---	---
6. Other Rods	0.7	2.4	1.5	1.3	1.7	1.4	2.6	1.8	2.5	2.8	1.7
7. Wire	4.5	3.9	0.9	3.2	1.3	1.9	1.5	1.6	1.2	0.7	0.5
8. Cable	0.5	0.6	0.6	0.5	0.4	0.3	0.2	0.2	0.1	0.2	0.5

9. Rails and Maintenance of Way	25.1	1.4	18.2	16.2	21.4	19.2	0.3	19.9	9.9	17.5	9.9
10. Pipe	11.4	20.5	9.7	5.6	4.4	4.0	1.5	3.1	3.5	3.0	2.9
11. Pipe Connections	0.4	---	0.1	0.2	0.3	0.4	0.2	0.7	0.6	0.6	0.4
12. Drainage	---	---	---	---	---	---	---	---	---	---	---
13. Structural Shapes	4.0	2.6	1.1	1.0	1.6	1.6	1.2	1.5	1.6	1.2	3.9
14. Spikes and Nails	---	---	---	---	0.2	0.1	0.1	0.2	0.2	0.2	0.2
15. Screws and Rivets	0.4	0.3	0.2	0.2	0.1	0.1	0.1	0.1	0.1	9.1	0.1
16. Chain	---	0.2	0.1	0.1	0.1	0.2	---	---	---	---	0.1
17. Iron and Steel Containers	0.8	0.3	0.2	0.6	0.9	0.6	0.6	0.6	0.2	1.0	0.4
18. Tin Cans	1.6	2.8	1.7	1.8	1.3	2.3	2.4	1.8	1.9	1.9	1.0

Source: Computed from data in Table 57.

TABLE 57

Imports of Steel Products by Country of Origin
(Thousands of Metric Tons)

Country	1913 (A)	(B)	1925 (A)	(B)	1929 (A)	(B)	1936 (A)	(B)	1937 (A)	(B)	1938 (A)	(B)	1950 (A)	(B)	1951 (A)	(B)
Austria	---	---	---	---	---	---	0.1	---	0.3	---	0.1	---	0.7	---	1.1	---
Belgium-Luxembourg	6.3	5	---	---	2.2	2	1.0	1	---	---	---	---	20.5	8	39.4	9
Canada	---	---	---	---	---	---	---	---	---	---	---	---	0.8	---	0.5	---
Czechoslovakia	---	---	---	---	---	---	1.2	1	---	---	---	---	---	---	---	---
France	---	---	---	---	---	---	---	---	2.0	1	0.4	1	6.5	3	26.1	6
Germany	13.5	10	6.6	7	9.7	8	30.2	27	31.6	15	9.1	17	25.9	10	120.8	28
Italy	---	---	---	---	---	---	---	---	---	---	---	---	---	---	---	---
Japan	---	---	---	---	---	---	---	---	20.0	10	---	---	---	---	---	---
Netherlands	---	---	---	---	0.3	---	---	---	---	---	---	---	---	---	0.1	---
Sweden	---	---	0.5	---	0.6	---	0.4	---	1.0	---	0.4	1	---	---	4.1	1
United Kingdom	13.2	10	8.5	9	23.5	18	18.5	17	17.3	8	7.2	14	8.2	3	1.3	---
United States	97.9	75	81.9	84	82.5	69	59.5	54	134.5	65	35.6	67	184.8	75	229.8	54
Total	130.9	100	97.5	100	118.8	100	110.9	100	206.7	100	52.8	100	247.4	100	424.5	100

	1952		1953		1954		1955		1956		1957		1958		1959	
	A	B	A	B	A	B	A	B	A	B	A	B	A	B	A	B
Austria	1.3	---	0.1	---	0.3	---	0.3	---	0.7	---	5.6	1	0.3	3	---	---
Belgium-Luxembourg	31.6	10	9.5	4	2.9	---	6.3	3	26.8	8	5.9	2	9.1	3	1.6	1
Canada	1.5	---	0.7	---	0.4	---	56.9	23	73.3	21	94.5	25	23.0	8	4.6	3
Czechoslovakia	---	---	---	---	4.7	2	---	---	---	---	---	---	---	---	---	---
France	7.3	2	20.8	8	36.3	17	26.1	11	19.2	6	19.3	5	25.8	9	25.2	15
Germany	22.1	7	9.2	3	26.2	12	31.6	13	28.3	8	31.1	8	28.4	10	23.6	14
Italy	0.1	---	---	---	20.5	9	28.7	12	32.8	9	46.6	12	17.9	6	---	---
Japan	13.0	4	3.1	1	6.3	3	8.3	3	1.0	---	0.6	---	---	---	5.4	3
Netherlands	---	---	---	---	---	---	---	---	3.5	---	---	---	0.1	---	---	---
Sweden	0.9	---	0.8	---	1.0	---	0.9	---	1.2	---	1.4	---	1.0	---	1.2	---
United Kingdom	0.6	---	1.3	---	1.3	---	2.7	1	3.0	1	2.0	---	7.0	2	7.6	5
United States	229.0	74	219.0	83	117.6	54	81.4	33	157.7	45	171.4	45	169.9	60	97.0	58
Total	307.4	100	264.5	100	217.5	100	243.2	100	347.5	100	378.4	100	282.5	100	166.2	100

Source: United Nations. *Statistics of World Trade in Steel.*
A = thousands of tons; B = percentage of total. Not all columns add to 100, due to rounding.

railroads and the better terms are often available from producers in the United States or Europe.[1] Flat-rolled products, none of which were produced in Mexico prior to the 1940's, now account for less than 5 per cent of steel imports. Pipe accounted for 20.5 per cent of total imports in 1954, but only 3.0 and 2.9 per cent in 1962 and 1963 respectively. The installation of TAMSA, together with the protective tariff, was instrumental in bringing about this reduction.

For three basic reasons it is not likely that the level of imports can be substantially reduced for some time to come. First, decisions have not been made to increase production of railway steel domestically; therefore, a significant volume of imports of this item can be expected to continue. Second, until Mexico reaches a significantly higher level of development and sustains that level, domestic scrap supplies will be inadequate for the growing steel industry. Third, there will be items of specialty that the domestic industry will not produce due to the limited size of market for these products.

While the United States has been the major supplier of Mexican steel imports, many nations have served as sources of supply—a fact illustrated by Table 57. The United States' proportion of total imports has remained large, but significant gains by Germany, France, Canada, and Italy will be noted. Most of the Canadian steel has been in the form of railway material, with these imports totalling 186,100 tons for the period 1955–1959.[2] Most of the balance of railway-steel imports originated in the United States. Most of the imports from Italy have been in the form of ingots, billets, or semifinished steel.[3]

Most of the imports of flat-rolled steel, sheet, plate, and tin plate have originated in the United States, as has also been the case with structural steel except for the period 1951–1953, when Belgium, France, and Luxembourg accounted for a significant portion.[4] As regards imports of pipes and fittings, the United States has been the major supplier, with France, Germany, and Italy making significant contributions.

At this point it may be appropriate to analyze imports from another aspect, that of the import-replacement policy. As explained

[1] Eduardo L. de la Torre Kuhn, *El Mercado Nacional de Carros de Ferrocarril,* p. 82.
[2] United Nations, *Statistics of World Trade in Steel,* n. p.
[3] *Ibid.*
[4] *Ibid.*

in Chapter 2, this policy was designed to supplant imports of steel with domestic steel. It carried the concomitant motive of conserving foreign exchange, with much of that savings to be used to import capital goods to aid in the implementation of the policy of industrialization. Table 58 indicates that imports of machinery and equipment have increased considerably during the period 1948–1962 and that this category of imports as a percentage of total has increased somewhat.

In Table 59 an attempt is made to estimate in terms of foreign exchange the cost that would have impinged on the economy if the investments in expansion of capacity between 1941 and 1963 had not been forthcoming. In using this technique, two basic assumptions are made: one, that steel production continued until 1962, at the level of the yearly average for the years 1941–1943; and two, that consumption of steel for the period 1947–1962 followed the same pattern as in fact it followed for that period.

TABLE 58

Imports of Machinery and Equipment
(Million of Pesos)

Year	Machinery and Equipment	Total Imports	Machinery and Equipment ÷ Total Imports %
1948	1,251.08	2,949.64	42.4
1949	1,499.51	3,524.29	42.5
1950	1,754.53	4,401.87	39.5
1951	2,896.99	6,576.16	44.1
1952	2,783.43	6,390.59	43.6
1953	2,693.13	6,350.03	42.4
1954	3,465.92	8,063.92	43.0
1955	4,359.16	11,045.73	39.5
1956	5,569.86	13,395.37	41.6
1957	5,947.98	14,439.47	41.2
1958	6,049.72	14,107.96	42.9
1959	5,701.63	12,582.66	45.3
1960	6,942.31	14,830.60	46.8
1961	6,777.83	14,232.39	47.6
1962	6,647.63	14,295.47	46.5

Source: United Nations, *Yearbook of International Trade Statistics.*

TABLE 59

Hypothetical Foreign Exchange Outlays for Steel in Absence of Import-Substitution Policy

	1947	1948	1949	1950	1951	1952	1953	1954
1. Consumption of Finished Products[a] (Thousands of metric tons)	562	433	491	591	803	759	680	698
2. Production (Thousands of tons) (1941–1943 average)	161	161	161	161	161	161	161	161
3. Necessity to Import (Thousands of tons) [1–2]	401	272	330	430	642	598	519	537
4. U.S. Price plus Freight[b] (U.S. dollars)	89.96	100.20	106.64	110.89	117.55	120.22	126.70	131.38
5. Outlay in Foreign Exchange (Millions of U.S. dollars) [3×4]	36.1	27.3	35.2	47.7	75.5	71.9	65.8	70.6
6. Per-Ton Cost of Imported Factors for Domestic Production (U.S. dollars)	26.60	30.42	32.75	34.23	36.64	37.50	39.83	41.47
7. Total Cost of Imported Factors (Millions of U.S. dollars)	10.6	8.3	10.8	14.7	23.5	22.4	20.7	22.3
8. Foreign Exchange Loss [5–7] (Millions of U.S. dollars)	25.5	19.0	24.4	33.0	52.0	49.5	45.1	48.3

	1955	1956	1957	1958	1959	1960	1961	1962
1. Consumption of Finished Products[a] (Thousands of metric tons)	854	1,176	1,285	1,217	1,139	1,392	1,422	1,424
2. Production (Thousands of tons) (1941–1943 average)	161	161	161	161	161	161	161	161
3. Necessity to Import (Thousands of tons) [1–2]	693	1,015	1,124	1,056	978	1,231	1,261	1,263
4. U.S. Price plus Freight[b] (U.S. dollars)	137.48	145.79	157.31	164.04	166.98	167.53	168.09	168.66
5. Outlay in Foreign Exchange (Millions of U.S. dollars) [3×4]	95.3	148.0	176.8	173.2	163.3	206.2	212.0	213.0
6. Per-Ton Cost of Imported Factors for Domestic Production (U.S. dollars)	43.65	46.68	50.57	53.37	54.30	54.30	54.30	54.30
7. Total Cost of Imported Factors (Millions of U.S. dollars)	30.2	47.4	56.8	56.4	53.1	66.8	68.5	68.6
8. Foreign Exchange Loss [5–7] (Millions of U.S. dollars)	65.1	100.6	120.0	116.8	110.2	139.3	143.5	144.4

[a] Figures for consumption in terms of ingots have been converted to consumption of finished products by applying the coefficient .7501.

[b] This is a composite price, weighted by product, for U.S. consumption. The weighting is similar to the breakdown of Mexican steel consumption, Table 21. To the composite price has been added transportation on the same basis as in Appendix A. Source of composite price: American Metal Market, *Metal Statistics 1963*, p. 211.

In Table 59, Item 3, "Necessity to Import," gives the level of imports that would have been required to sustain the level of consumption shown in Item 1. Item 5, "Outlay in Foreign Exchange," represents the amount of foreign exchange that would have been required to purchase the quantities of steel represented in Item 3. The figures for cost of imported factors (Item 6) were computed by using the "Cost of Imported Factors" figure from Table 12. This figure of $30.32 was pegged as base for the year 1948 and the figures for the preceding year and succeeding years have been varied in proportion with changes in price of steel imports (Item 4). Since the major proportion of outlay for foreign factors goes for capital equipment, it seems that this procedure of varying factor costs would give a close approximation. A major shortcoming of the figures in Item 6 is that no allowance has been made for economies of scale.

If, in fact, economies of scale were enjoyed by the industry as production increased, figures for each year's per-ton cost of foreign factors would be less than those shown.

The foreign exchange loss would have surpassed $100 million in each of the years from 1956 through 1963, and the total outlay would have risen to more than $200 million, given the stated assumptions and in the absence of the import substitution that took place.

The build-up of steel's productive capacity with its accompanying economies of scale, together with external economies derived from Mexico's general economic growth has allowed the Mexican steel industry to enter into competition for export outlets. In the preceding chapter it was noted that many of the steel products produced in Mexico have showed trends with declining rates of growth. It is possible, however, that the export market can be exploited sufficiently to sustain the present rate of growth for the industry for some time into the future.

Table 60 lists exports by product type for the years 1953 through 1963. Finished products have accounted for most of Mexico's exports, with the exception of 1961 when 46,000 tons of pig iron were exported. Exports of finished products have grown steadily, so that for 1963 exports totaled 171,313 tons, a figure larger than the 158,-170 tons of imported finished steel products. Sheet steel and pipe have accounted for the bulk of exports. Sheet steel became a factor

TABLE 60
Exports of Steel Products from Mexico (Metric Tons)

	1953	1954	1955	1956	1957	1958	1959	1960	1961	1962	1963
Primary Materials	29	...	1,326	3,233	4,539	410	3	65	48,729	12,225	5,868
1. Scrap	29	...	29	13	1,495	...	1	57	16	2,225	1,420
2. Pig Iron	...	...	...	...	...	9	...	8	46,096	264	8
3. Ingots	...	...	2	3	...	...	...	...	1	6,978	259
4. Alloys	...	...	1,295	3,217	3,044	401	2	...	2,616	2,840	4,181
Finished Steel Products	604	1,547	3,473	8,380	12,168	4,873	21,032	19,435	28,908	44,778	171,313
1. Sheet	...	25	106	30	5	20	2,915	1,920	5,565	22,479	112,049
2. Tinplate	...	41	2	...	...	...	...	7	35	798	3,167
3. Strips	...	...	7	123	58	10	345	156	170	114	469
4. Rods for concrete	...	22	503	231	88	61	7,872	9,670	4,667	4	4
5. Other Rods	1	3	8	12	6	3	990	73	20	30	36
6. Wire	...	4	7	20	67	1,140	2,282	1,794	406	98	86
7. Cable	...	7	4	5	33	15	5	1	6	3	129
8. Pipe	152	341	1,874	5,444	7,587	124	1,033	569	13,089	14,889	48,505
9. Pipe Connections	...	...	...	...	312	1,417	...	1,933	2,406	3,190	3,661
10. Drainage Pipe	...	...	...	...	...	...	...	...	...	...	...
11. Structural Shapes	220	51	80	149	86	61	2,885	373	23	56	251
12. Spikes and Nails	2	3	14	129	82	186	123	152	149	41	93
13. Chain	4	16	10	22	6	3	45	5	1	77	...
14. Iron and Steel Containers	214	1,026	538	1,203	702	586	1,258	1,534	1,366	2,041	1,651
15. Tin Cans	11	8	320	1,109	1,132	1,257	1,279	1,248	917	958	1,212
Total	633	1,547	4,799	11,613	16,707	5,283	21,035	19,500	77,637	57,003	177,181

Source: Cámara Nacional del Hierro y del Acero, *Circular No. 19.*

in exports in 1959 and the price of domestic production fell relative to United States prices for that product.

Total steel exports for 1963 were 177,181 tons, more than 300 per cent of 1962 exports—a magnitude that was probably unexpected. A prediction made by NAFIN in June of 1963 estimated conservatively that exports would approach 200,000 tons in 1970.[5]

Much of the pipe exports have gone to markets in the United States. Recently, the Tennessee Gas Transmission Company contracted with Nacional Tubacero, S.A., for pipe to be used in a pipeline to run between Texas and California.[6]

In addition to exports of steel products, exports of products that are steel intensive have been significant. Reference is made especially to export of railroad cars to the United States. The Constructora Nacional de Carros de Ferrocarril recently sold one hundred boxcars to the Missouri-Pacific railroad and has sold some few cars in Central America.[7] Mexico would appear to have a cost advantage over boxcar producers in the United States. The following schedule compares the cost of producing a boxcar in three areas in 1956:

Mexico (Constructora Nacional) $7,900
United States 8,457
Europe .... 8,200[8]

Each boxcar contains about nine tons of steel, including steel plate for roof and skirting, steel sections for the underframe, and forgings for wheels and axles.[9] While the cars have a high steel content this does not mean that only domestic steel has been used in their production. In the first production run (1955), 80 per cent of all materials consumed were imported.[10] By 1957 imports had been cut to 56 per cent and plans were made for even more drastic cuts in importation of inputs.

The promotion of steel exports falls within the broad export policy of the Mexican government:

It is part of Mexico's foreign trade policy to encourage the export of products with as high a degree of manufacturing as possible. This is

[5] Nacional Financiera, S.A., *El Mercado de Valores*, June 3, 1963.
[6] *El Universal*, December 3, 1963, n. p.
[7] Dale B. Truett, *Development of Transport Equipment Industry*.
[8] Constructora Nacional de Carros de Ferrocarril, S.A., *Furgones*, p. 33.
[9] United Nations, *Railways and Steel*, p. iii.
[10] Constructora Nacional de Carros de Ferrocarril, S.A., *Informe Anual*, 1955, p. 12.

partly due to the jobs, salaries and other benefits these goods provide at home, and higher prices and better conditions of sale they command abroad than do raw materials.[11]

In practical form this policy expresses itself in several ways. The Mexican government sends trade missions to seek out markets, and works with the Inter-American Development Bank and through its own facilities to finance exports. In 1964 the Banco de Comercio Exterior began to grant credit to importers in Central America to cover purchase of Mexican manufactures and semimanufactures.[12] Also, the government is active in negotiating the reduction of trade barriers among the LAFTA signatories.

A market for Mexican steel exports may well develop in Latin America and such development may be helped by the Latin American Free Trade Association (LAFTA). By promoting a lowering of tariff barriers among the signatories while retaining a barrier to the rest of the world, LAFTA is utilizing the infant-industry argument on a regional scale. This argument was also vocalized by the Latin American Iron and Steel Institute at its recent Congress held in Mexico City in July, 1964. The following is quoted from that meeting:

El costo de producción es más elevado en la América Latina que en los países industrializados y para proteger a su industria, los gobiernos tendrán que recurrir a las barreras arancelarias, pero el problema será más agudo si su producción ha llegado a un volúmen elevado que no solamente llene sus necesidades internas, sino que dejar un exedente que tampoco podrían colocar en el exterior salvo sacrificando precios.[13]

Thus, according to the Latin American Iron and Steel Institute, trade barriers must be constructed to protect the infant industries in Latin America from competition from the industrially developed countries, but barriers are to be reduced among the Latin American nations so that industries can enjoy larger markets, thus taking advantage of economies of scale. But the Latin American market is not large enough to support six or seven steel industries in competition with each other. It is not considered sufficient that the internal market of each country be preserved for that country's industry, but

---

[11] Banco Nacional de Comercio Exterior, S.A., *Comercio Exterior* (English edition), May, 1965, p. 16.

[12] *Ibid.*, p. 5.

[13] *Negocios*, July, 1964, p. 1.

so that economies of scale may be enjoyed, the barriers between countries are to be reduced, thus widening the potential market.

The problem is to avoid competition among the various Latin American steel producers and at the same time permit each steel mill to enjoy economies of scale. This dual purpose could be accomplished by a division of LAFTA markets among the major steel producers so that by each concentrating on a narrow range of products, economies of scale could be enjoyed.

El problema grande a resolver radica en la coordinación de la producción (de acero), asignado de común acuerdo, a cada país determinados tipos de aceros para producirlos en gran volumen. En esta forma cada país podría bajar sus costos y contaría con un mercado interno y de exportación lo suficiente grande para justicificar el ensanchamiento de sus plantas y la adopción de las técnicas más avanzadas.[14]

This problem was discussed at the 1964 meeting of the Latin American Institute of Iron and Steel in Mexico City; however, the political processes have not yet provided the machinery necessary to promulgate such a scheme. Further, there is some doubt that countries like Mexico and Brazil, who have large steel industries in operation, would be content to give up production of types of steel for which they already have installed capacity.

Although no concrete steps have been taken regarding division of production among the various steel industries, the reduction of tariff barriers among the LAFTA countries has begun. As of the end of 1963, 8,248 tariff concessions had been made, with a large percentage of these covering basic metals and their manufactures.[15] These reductions have had an apparent effect on the level of Mexican exports, as attested by Table 61.

Steel products have been included among exports of manufactured goods, but the total is not here presented. Other data does give some idea as to the growing importance of steel in Mexico's LAFTA export mix. In Table 62 steel products are shown as among those registering the largest export increases.

While some progress has been made by LAFTA, "there is evidently a wide gap between the good intentions manifested on the surface and the conclusion of the necessary agreements."[16] One

[14] *Ibid.*, p. 2.
[15] Banco Nacional, *Comercio Exterior*, November, 1964, p. 760.
[16] *Ibid.*, October, 1964, p. 5.

TABLE 61

Mexican Exports to LAFTA Countries
(Millions of Pesos)

Export	1962	1963	1964
Food, Drink, and Tobacco	7.9	12.3	35.9
Raw Materials	63.1	70.0	127.8
Chemicals	21.5	57.4	51.5
Manufactured Goods Including Machinery	208.0	324.9	413.1

Source: Banco Nacional de Comercio Exterior, S.A., *Comercio Exterior*, January, 1965, p. 4.

would be hasty to conclude that it is always pressure from private business that slows LAFTA's machinery. A case to prove the opposite is that of the machine-tool industry. Major machine manufacturers of Argentina, Brazil and Mexico recommended to their respective governments more than one hundred tariff concessions designed to promote complementarity in the industry. Of the total concessions recommended by the manufacturers, only two were added to the free trade list during the Bogotá negotiations in 1964.[17]

Further, the Inter-American Development Bank whose directors

TABLE 62

Major 1963 Exports to LAFTA Countries Registering Growth over 1962

Product	Increment (millions of pesos)
Steel Sheet and Plate	29.2
Steel Pipe	16.9
Sodium Phosphate	14.6
Books	8.5
Metal Cable	8.0
Industrial Specialties	7.0
Cotton	6.6
Tinplate	6.3

Source: Banco Nacional de Comercio Exterior, S.A., *Comercio Exterior*, February, 1964.

[17] *Ibid.* (English edition), May, 1965, p. 16.

have announced their desire to promote economic integration "does not seem disposed to provide the modest financing" for recommended studies for complementary industries among the LAFTA countries.[18]

Although geographic proximity to the United States and treaty ties with LAFTA countries make these more susceptible to Mexican exports, Mexico is overlooking no area of the world in its quests for markets. In 1964 the Banco Nacional de Comercio Exterior, S.A. sent four trade missions abroad with only one of them visiting the LAFTA countries. One mission visited the republics of the Central American Common Market and Panama while another visited Japan, Hong Kong, and the China Mainland. The fourth mission worked in Yugoslavia, Poland, Czechoslovakia, and the Soviet Union. The objective of each mission was the exploration of opportunities for foreign markets for Mexican goods.

On the surface it might appear that there would be no opportunity for sale of Mexican steel in such areas as those on the fringe of industrial Europe, but in 1963 Yugoslavia purchased $729,682 (Mexican currency) of structural steel products from Mexican producers, and a small quantity of flat-rolled steel products was shipped to Italy. Although the tonnage then involved was small, the potential market may well circle the globe.

Some phraseology from a NAFIN publication may give a hint as to why a developing country's steel products may be able to compete for export markets with what may be more efficient mills in Germany and France. In speaking of the probability of increased steel exports, NAFIN lists one reason as "the flexible politics of export prices." It has long been recognized that industries having high fixed capital costs and not enjoying sufficient domestic demand to operate at capacity, may seek to increase their level of output by selling on the export market at some price lower than their price on the domestic market.[19] Theoretically, the export price could be somewhere below average cost and "any income above differential cost clear gain," as fixed costs would be covered by the domestic price.[20]

If this is what NAFIN is hinting at when it refers to "the flexible politics of export prices," it may be that in a country such as Mexico

---

[18] *Ibid.*

[19] Irwin Hexner, *The International Steel Cartel*, pp. 29; 172–3.

[20] John Maurice Clark, *Studies in the Economics of Overhead Costs*, p. 178.

with a fairly advanced steel industry, with raw materials available domestically, and wages relatively low, the variable cost of producing steel is sometimes lower than in highly industrialized countries.

9. Conclusion

The Mexican iron and steel industry is now a strong and integral part of the Mexican economy. That the Mexican government played a major role in its building cannot be doubted. The tariff wall that implemented the government's policy of import replacement allowed the domestic industry to absorb a major portion of the domestic market and improve its price position relative to that of the United States. That position has improved to the extent that Mexico is exporting significant amounts of steel. Other forms of government aid, such as tax concessions, direct investment, and aid in financing have helped the industry.

For all steel products except rails and maintenance of way material, domestic production has accounted for an increasing proportion of steel consumption. Large amounts of sheet steel and steel pipe have been exported recently and in 1963, production of sheet exceeded domestic consumption. For the past two decades the rate of growth of steel production has been significantly higher than that of steel consumption; however, as the level of production approaches that of consumption, the difference in growth rates will decline. Failing an increase in the rate of growth of consumption, the recent trend of production can be sustained only by a substantial increase in exports. While there have been substantial increases in exports in the past few years, it is as yet too early to assume that a trend has been established. Much of the answer to the question of export markets will depend on political developments within LAFTA.

As would seem proper, growth of steel consumption is tied to growth of the economy in general. In Chapter 6 the point was made that output in most industrial sectors is becoming more steel-intensive. With the assumption that present economic trends will continue for the remainder of the decade, it was projected that steel consumption for the year 1970 would reach 3,388,000 tons (ingots).

Any significant change in the growth rate of GNP would probably cause somewhat similar changes in the growth of steel consumption.

The growth of the steel industry has led to growth in those industries that are backwardly linked to steel. Domestic coal mines supply all of the coking coal used by the steel industry and iron-ore production moves *pari passu* with pig-iron production. In addition to these basic and more well-known inputs, limestone, ferroalloys, refractory bricks, natural gas, fuel oil, and electricity have been subjected to steel's backward-linkage pull. Included in the backward-linkage effect has been rail transportation, which for a while formed a bottleneck between the steel industry and its suppliers of raw materials. The demand for rail cars by steel and allied industries accounted for part of the "pull effect" leading to the establishment of a plant for the production of rail cars, and the existence of domestic steel plate probably was a consideration favoring establishment of Constructora Nacional. One dark shadow on the backward-linkage horizon is that of scrap iron and steel. The domestic supply of scrap is limited and much of the demand for this item is expended on imports.

Since 1940 much of the sequence of investments in Mexican steel and linked industries fit rather well into a Hirschman pattern of forced and induced decision making. The original plans for AHMSA, as drawn up by private entreprenuers, called for a small nonintegrated operation using imported semifinished steel. The Mexican government did not want Mexican steel production tied to foreign raw materials and was "forced" to enter into partnership with the private interests. By joint effort they planned and financed AHMSA as an integrated operation. The integrated mill originally had much excess capacity, which may have been a factor leading to government decisions to manufacture rail cars. Further, to a large extent, the idle capacity was due to a shortage of transportation facilities and this shortage "forced" the purchase of more rail cars which in turn was added inducement for decisions to invest in the manufacture of railroad rolling stock. Demand for coke on the part of the growing steel industry led to investments in coke production, which brought with it the production of chemical and fertilizers as by-products.

Import substitution for the most important steel products is nearly complete, but a large range of industrial and consumer imports cover manufactured products with significant steel content. In some of these areas—most notably automobiles, trucks, and buses—a program of import substitution is already being implemented. In others, such as railway rolling stock, import substitution has been completed, boxcars are being exported, and plans have been proposed to promote the sale of machine tools in LAFTA countries. The fact that the steel industry is now well established probably offers added encouragement for the Mexican government to promote import replacement for products that include large quantities of steel. The present program for domestic production of motor vehicles might have been much less attractive without the forward-linkage effects of the domestic supplies of steel. Without domestic steel, the replacement of automobile imports would require increases in steel imports.

Further, it is possible that the level of foreign exchange earnings would not comfortably support the existing level of steel consumption if most of present-day steel requirements had to be imported. It is also possible that there would have been fewer decisions in the private sector to invest in industries that consume large quantities of steel if inputs were dependent on the fluctuating level of foreign-exchange earnings.

The steel industry is now big, strong, and diversified. Production has grown fourfold since 1944 and more than doubled in the period 1954 to 1963. While market considerations may place a ceiling on its growth, there is little question of its continued importance. Whether the Mexican steel industry could survive in open competition with the steel industries of the more industrialized countries may be questionable, but the Mexican government undoubtedly would not let foreign competition jeopardize the industry in which its "showcase of public intervention (AHMSA)" forms the capstone.

Appendices

Domestic Prices, Costs of Imports, and Tariffs for Flat-rolled Products

TABLE 63

Computation of Level of Tariff Barrier for Selected Steel Products (1944–1962)

(Cost per Ton)

	1944	1945	1946	1947	1948	1949	1950
Tinplate							
1). Price in U.S. (dollars)[a]	110.23	110.23	110.23	126.76	149.91	170.86	165.35
2). Price in U.S. (pesos)[b]	535.50	535.50	535.50	615.42	836.95	1,318.78	1,430.27
3). Transportation Costs[c]	98.71	100.70	102.70	104.67	122.83	173.12	198.02
4). Specific Tariff[d]	200.00	200.00	200.00	200.00	150.00	100.00	100.00
5). Ad Valorem Tariff[d]	......	......	......	......	251.09	329.55	350.07
6). Total Barrier (2, 3, 4, 5)	834.21	836.20	838.20	920.09	1,360.87	1,920.85	2,078.36
Plate							
1). Price in U.S. (dollars)[a]	46.30	49.16	54.45	61.07	70.11	75.84	77.60
2). Price in U.S. (pesos)[b]	224.93	238.82	264.52	296.50	391.42	585.11	671.24
3). Transportation Costs[c]	98.71	100.70	102.70	104.67	122.83	173.12	198.02
4). Specific Tariff[d]	250.00	250.00	250.00	250.00	100.00	100.00	100.00
5). Ad Valorem Tariff[d]	......	......	......	......	117.43	146.28	167.81
6). Total Barrier (2, 3, 4, 5)	573.64	589.52	617.22	651.17	731.68	1,004.51	1,137.07
Sheet							
1). Price in U.S. (dollars)[a]	70.55	70.55	74.96	79.37	87.74	93.70	96.34
2). Price in U.S. (pesos)[b]	342.73	342.73	364.18	385.34	489.85	722.90	833.34
3). Transportation Costs[c]	98.71	100.70	102.70	104.67	133.83	173.12	198.02
4). Specific Tariff[d]	250.00	250.00	250.00	250.00	100.00	100.00	100.00
5). Ad Valorem Tariff[d]	......	......	......	......	146.95	180.73	208.34
6). Total Barrier (2, 3, 4, 5)	691.44	693.43	716.86	740.01	870.63	1,176.75	1,339.70

	1951	1952	1953	1954	1955	1956
Tinplate						
1). Price in U.S. (dollars)[a]	191.80	191.80	197.31	197.31	199.51	208.33
2). Price in U.S. (pesos)[b]	1,659.07	1,659.07	1,706.73	2,466.38	2,493.88	2,604.13
3). Transportation Costs[c]	202.00	206.07	210.20	309.75	316.00	322.38
4). Specific Tariff[d]	100.00	100.00	100.00	100.00	100.00	100.00
5). Ad Valorem Tariff[d]	414.77	414.77	426.68	616.60	623.40	651.03
6). Total Barrier (2, 3, 4, 5)	2,375.84	2,379.91	2,443.61	3,492.73	3,533.28	3,677.54
Plate						
1). Price in U.S. (dollars)[a]	81.57	83.55	88.18	91.71	96.12	102.29
2). Price in U.S. (pesos)[b]	705.58	722.71	762.76	1,146.38	1,201.50	1,278.63
3). Transportation Costs[c]	202.00	206.07	210.20	309.75	316.00	322.38
4). Specific Tariff[d]	300.00	300.00	300.00	520.00	520.00	520.00
5). Ad Valorem Tariff[d]	70.56	72.27	76.28	11.46	12.02	12.79
6). Total Barrier (2, 3, 4, 5)	1,278.14	1,301.05	1,349.24	1,987.59	2,049.52	2,133.80
Sheet						
1). Price in U.S. (dollars)[a]	101.41	103.62	107.14	115.96	121.91	130.07
2). Price in U.S. (pesos)[b]	877.20	896.31	926.76	1,449.50	1,523.88	1,625.88
3). Transportation Costs[c]	202.00	206.07	210.20	309.75	316.00	322.38
4). Specific Tariff[d]	300.00	300.00	300.00	520.00	520.00	520.00
5). Ad Valorem Tariff[d]	87.72	89.63	92.68	14.50	15.24	16.26
6). Total Barrier (2, 3, 4, 5)	1,466.92	1,492.01	1,529.64	2,293.75	2,375.12	2,484.52

[a] American Metal Market, *Metal Statistics 1963*.
[b] See Table 65 for conversion factors.
[c] United Nations, *A Study of the Iron and Steel Industry in Latin America*, I, 120. Ocean freight for 1948 was $12 per ton and cost of shipping steel from Pittsburgh to port was an additional $10. To this total of $22 per ton an increase of 2 per cent per annum was added for succeeding years and a 2-per cent decrease for preceding years.
[d] See Chapter 2 for tariff schedules.

TABLE 63—(Continued)

	1957	1958	1959	1960	1961	1962
Tinplate						
1). Price in U.S. (dollars)[a]	227.07	227.07	234.79	234.79	234.79	234.79
2). Price in U.S. (pesos)[b]	2,838.38	2,838.38	2,838.38	2,934.88	2,934.88	2,934.88
3). Transportation Costs[c]	328.88	335.50	342.25	349.13	356.13	363.25
4). Specific Tariff[d]	100.00	100.00	100.00	100.00	100.00	100.00
5). Ad Valorem Tariff[d]	709.60	709.60	733.72	733.72	733.72	733.72
6). Total Barrier (2, 3, 4, 5)	3,976.86	3,983.48	4,014.35	4,117.73	4,124.73	4,131.85
Plate						
1). Price in U.S. (dollars)[a]	109.57	114.20	116.84	116.84	116.84	116.84
2). Price in U.S. (pesos)[b]	1,369.63	1,427.50	1,460.50	1,460.50	1,460.50	1,460.50
3). Transportation Costs[c]	328.88	334.50	342.25	349.13	356.13	363.25
4). Specific Tariff[d]	520.00	550.00	550.00	550.00	550.00	550.00
5). Ad Valorem Tariff[d]	13.70	28.55	29.21	29.21	29.21	29.21
6). Total Barrier (2, 3, 4, 5)	2,232.21	2,341.55	2,381.96	2,388.84	2,395.84	2,402.96
Sheet						
1). Price in U.S. (dollars)[a]	139.99	145.50	148.37	148.37	148.37	148.37
2). Price in U.S. (pesos)[b]	1,749.88	1,818.75	1,854.63	1,854.63	1,854.63	1,854.63
3). Transportation Costs[c]	328.88	335.50	342.25	349.13	356.13	363.25
4). Specific Tariff[d]	520.00	550.00	550.00	550.00	550.00	550.00
5). Ad Valorem Tariff[d]	17.50	36.37	37.09	37.09	37.09	37.09
6). Total Barrier (2, 3, 4, 5)	2,616.26	2,740.62	2,783.97	2,790.85	2,799.85	2,804.97

TABLE 64

Domestic Prices for Flat-Rolled Steel Products (1947–1962)[a]
(Pesos per Metric Ton)

Year	Sheet	Plate	Tin Plate
1947	562	460	1,171
1948	817	548	1,385
1949	952	726	1,665
1950	------	------	------
1951	1,033	814	1,819
1952	1,056	833	1,901
1953	1,292	987	2,021
1954	1,708	1,343	2,073
1955	1,751	1,691	2,432
1956	1,942	1,597	2,786
1957	2,237	1,796	3,314
1958	2,173	1,721	3,351
1959	2,135	1,729	3,293
1960	2,081	1,772	3,477
1961	2,003	1,557	3,385
1962	2,057	1,658	3,275

Source: Dirección General de Estadística, *Revista Estadística*, 1947–1963.
[a] Obtained by dividing data for yearly value by tons of output.

TABLE 65

Exchange Rate of Mexican Pesos for U.S. Dollars (1944–1962)
(Import Rate in Pesos per U.S. Dollar)

Year	Rate	Year	Rate
1944	4.858	1954	12.50
1945	4.858	1955	12.50
1946	4.855	1956	12.50
1947	5.583	1957	12.50
1948	7.715	1958	12.50
1949	3.650	1959	12.50
1950	8.650	1960	12.50
1951	8.650	1961	12.50
1952	8.650	1962	12.50
1953	8.650		

Source: International Monetary Fund, *Balance of Payments Yearbook*.

Appendix B

Estimated Costs for a Hypothetical Plant in Monclova, Coahuila

The Economic Commission for Latin America has furnished cost data for various plants in Latin America, some of which are hypothetical.[1] The cost figures in Table 15 were derived from four tables in this study. The United Nations' study considered only one level of production for Mexico's Monclova plant, that of an annual capacity of 430,000 tons. In order to demonstrate the effect of the level of production on economies of scale, it was necessary to have cost data for various levels of capacity. The above-mentioned study did provide such figures for a hypothetical plant in Venezuela (Barcelona). These figures are reproduced in Table 66. Costs were based upon classical methods of ore reduction and steel making.[2] Classical methods employed were similar to those in Mexico's Monclova plant; therefore, it is assumed that wage and capital costs in Monclova will vary by the same proportions as the cost figures in Table 66. The percentage variation has been computed by using 430,000 tons as a base, selected because cost figures available for the Monclova plant are based on a capacity of 430,000 tons. The Venezuelan data is not used to quantify the model because, as shown in the United Nations' study, labor costs in Venezuela are by far the highest in Latin America and are far out of line with labor costs in the other Latin American steel industries.

Table 67 gives a breakdown of costs at Monclova on the basis of process involved and based upon a capacity of 430,000 tons of finished steel annually.

To compute the capital and labor costs for production of one ton of finished steel so as to include all costs, from pig-iron production to production of finished steel, some adjustments are necessary because less than one ton of pig iron is used to make a ton of ingot steel but 1.333 tons of ingot steel are used to make one ton of finished

[1] United Nations, *A Study of the Iron and Steel Industry in Latin America*, I.
[2] *Ibid.*, p. 23.

TABLE 66

Cost Differentials in Plants of Various Capacities at Barcelona
(In 1948 Dollars Per Ton of Steel)

Plant Capacity (Thousands of tons annually)	Wages	Capital Charges	Wage Index	Capital Index
50	49.79	44.20	275.5	133.1
150	33.41	42.20	184.9	127.1
200	26.91	40.60	148.9	122.3
230	23.01	37.40	127.3	112.7
300	20.80	34.70	115.0	104.5
430	18.07	33.20	100.0	100.0
716	15.73	30.80	87.1	92.8
850	15.60	31.90	86.3	96.1

Source: United Nations, *A Study of the Iron and Steel Industry in Latin America*, I.

TABLE 67

Breakdown of Costs at Monclova[a]
(In 1948 Dollars Per Ton)

	Pig-Iron Production	Steel-Ingot Production	Finished-Steel Production
Wages and Salaries	0.52	2.02	3.60
Capital Charges	8.28	5.10	18.00

Source: United Nations, *A Study of the Iron and Steel Industry in Latin America*, I.

[a] Based on a capacity of 430,000 tons annually.

steel.[3] The amount of pig iron used to make one ton of steel ingot can be obtained by dividing the cost of one ton of pig iron ($34.09) by the cost of the amount of pig iron used as an input in the production of one ton of ingot steel ($25.87).[4] The resulting percentage is .759, which represents a coefficient that can be applied to labor and capital costs of one ton of pig iron to determine how much of such costs should be counted in the production of one ton of ingot steel.

[3] *Ibid.*, p. 123.
[4] *Ibid.*, pp. 122–123.

The previously mentioned coefficient of 1.333 is applied to the labor and capital costs of producing one ton of steel ingot, as the production of one ton of finished steel requires 1.333 tons of steel ingot. By making these adjustments, the total labor and capital cost of producing a ton of finished steel can be computed from the data in Table 67. (see Table 68).

By applying the percentages for the wage index and the capital index (Table 66) to the "Total" figures in Table 68, hypothetical costs for the Monclova plant may be obtained, as shown below.

According to the United Nations study, the total cost of producing one ton of finished steel at the Monclova plant was $83.10; therefore, the difference between the total cost and cost of labor plus capital is $45.36. This figure of $45.36 is accounted for, in the main, by raw materials and fuel; if it is assumed that no economies of scale are to be involved with any of the costs other than capital and

TABLE 68

Breakdown of Costs of Finished Steel at Monclova
(Per Ton)

	Pig-Iron Production	Steel-Ingot Production	Finished-Steel Production	Total
Wages and Salaries	0.39	2.69	3.60	6.68
Capital Charges	6.28	6.78	18.00	31.06

TABLE 69

Hypothetical Wage and Capital Costs at Mexico's Monclova Plant
at Various Capacities
(In 1948 Dollars Per Ton)

Plant Capacity	Wages	Wage Index	Capital Cost	Capital Index
50,000	18.40	275.5	41.34	133.1
150,000	12.35	184.9	39.48	127.1
200,000	9.95	148.9	37.99	122.3
230,000	8.50	127.3	35.00	112.7
300,000	7.68	115.0	32.45	104.5
430,000	6.68	100.0	31.06	100.0
716,000	5.82	87.1	28.82	92.8
850,000	5.77	86.3	29.84	96.1

labor, $45.36 can be added to the unit cost at each level of production, thus arriving at a schedule of total unit cost.

TABLE 70

Hypothetical Unit Cost of Finished Steel at Monclova
(In 1948 Dollars Per Ton)

Plant Capacity	Wage Cost	Capital Cost	Other Costs	Total
50,000	18.40	41.34	45.36	105.10
150,000	12.35	39.48	45.36	97.19
200,000	9.95	37.99	45.36	93.30
230,000	8.50	35.00	45.36	88.86
300,000	7.68	32.45	45.36	85.49
430,000	6.68	31.06	45.36	83.10
716,000	5.82	28.82	45.36	80.00
850,000	5.77	29.84	45.36	80.97

Appendix C

Data for Correlations

1) Correlation of Mexican Gross National Product (1939–1960) with aggregate steel production in Mexico (1939–1960)
   GNP data taken from Chapter 5
   Steel-production data taken from Chapter 5

Coefficient A	$=-$	612,488.40000
Coefficient B	$=$	11,487.30500
Standard Error of Estimate	$=$	117,175.84000
Coefficient of Determination	$=$	0.91374
Coefficient of Correlation	$=$	0.95590
Value of T	$=$	14.55524

   Where X = GNP
   and Y = steel production

2) Correlation of Mexican Gross National Product (1939–1960) with aggregate steel consumption in Mexico (1939–1960)
   GNP data from Chapter 5
   Steel consumption data from Chapter 5

Coefficient A	$=-$	187,029.86000
Coefficient B	$=$	10,010.19400
Standard Error of Estimate	$=$	313,514.84000
Coefficient of Determination	$=$	0.52910
Coefficient of Correlation	$=$	0.72740
Value of T	$=$	4.74049

   Where X = GNP
   and Y = steel consumption

3) Correlation of index of industrial production with index of steel consumption for the years 1953–1961
   Index of industrial production from Chapter 6
   Index of steel consumption computed from data in Chapter 5

Coefficient A	$=-$	40.476940
Coefficient B	$=$	1.454699
Standard Error of Estimate	$=$	13.910000

Coefficient of Determination	=	0.879750
Coefficient of Correlation	=	0.937950
Value of T	=	7.156350

Where X = Index of industrial production
and Y = Index of steel consumption

4) Correlation of index of manufacturing production with index of steel consumption by the manufacturing sector for the years 1953–1961

Data taken from Table 31 and Table 32

Coefficient A	= −	65.744640
Coefficient B	=	1.707498
Standard Error of Estimate	=	12.440000
Coefficient of Determination	=	0.925370
Coefficient of Correlation	=	0.961960
Value of T	=	9.316720

Where X = Index of manufacturing production
and Y = Index of steel consumption by manufacturing sector

5) Correlation of mining production index with index of steel consumption by the mining sector, 1953–1961

Data taken from Tables 31 and 32

Coefficient A	= −	202.252760
Coefficient B	=	3.149330
Standard Error of Estimate	=	11.790000
Coefficient of Determination	=	0.720240
Coefficient of Correlation	=	0.848670
Value of T	=	4.24516

Where X = Index of mining production
and Y = Index of steel consumption by the mining sector

6) Correlation of petroleum production index with consumption of steel by the petroleum sector, 1953–1961

Data taken from Tables 31 and 32

Coefficient A	=	67.936730
Coefficient B	=	0.652590
Standard Error of Estimate	=	27.090000
Coefficient of Determination	=	0.558810
Coefficient of Correlation	=	0.747540
Value of T	=	2.977630

Where X = Index of petroleum production
and Y = Index of steel consumption by the petroleum sector

7) Correlation of construction production index with index of steel
   consumption by the construction sector for the years 1953–1961
   Data taken from Tables 31 and 32

Coefficient A	=	93.631770
Coefficient B	=	1.962304
Standard Error of Estimate	=	6.432000
Coefficient of Determination	=	0.982300
Coefficient of Correlation	=	0.991110
Value of T	=	19.710300

   Where X = Index of construction production
   and Y = Index of consumption of steel by construction sector

8) Correlation of Mexican coal production with Mexican pig-iron
   production for the years 1939–1960
   Data for coal production from Table 46
   and for pig-iron production from Table 71

Coefficient A	=	659.403200
Coefficient B	=	1.904309
Standard Error of Estimate	=	131.190000
Coefficient of Determination	=	0.756390
Coefficient of Correlation	=	0.869700
Value of T	=	7.880170

   Where X = Pig-iron production
   and Y = Coal production

TABLE 71

Mexican Pig-Iron Production
(Thousands of Tons)

Year	Tons	Year	Tons
1939	141	1950	227
1940	92	1951	213
1941	95	1952	238
1942	122	1953	242
1943	159	1954	237
1944	159	1955	312
1945	210	1956	409
1946	240	1957	414
1947	236	1958	478
1948	276	1959	473
1949	206	1960	530

Sources: Cámara Nacional de la Industria del Hierro y del Acero: *Tercer Congreso*; Nacional Financiera, S.A., *Informal Anual, 1964*.

Bibliography

OFFICIAL PUBLICATIONS

Mexico

Banco de México, S.A. *Aceros, Notas sobre su Fabricación, Caraterísticas y Clasificación.* México, D.F., 1961.
————. *La Industria Siderúrgica de México.* México, D.F., 1961.
Banco Nacional de Comercio Exterior, S.A. *Comercio Exterior de México* (English edition), May, 1963, México, D.F.
————. *Comercio Exterior,* February, 1964; October, 1964; and November, 1964, México, D.F.
————. *Informe Especial: La Industria Siderúrgica.* México, D.F., n.d.
Dirección General de Estadística. *Compendio Estadístico 1960.* México, D.F., 1962.
Nacional Financiera, S.A. *Informe Anual, 1963.* México, D.F., 1963.
————. *Informe Anual, 1964.* México, D.F., 1964.
————. *El Mercado de Valores,* Vol. XXIII, No. 22, México, D.F.
————. *Estadísticas Económicas de México.* México, D.F., 1963.
————. *Las Corporaciones de Fomento de la Producción.* México, D.F., 1946.
Secretaría de Comunicaciones y Transportes. *Estadística de Ferrocarriles y Tranvías de 1962.* México, D.F.: Talleres Gráficas de la Nacion, 1963.
Secretaría de Economía. *La Economía Mexicana en 1957.* México, D.F., 1958.
Secretaría de Industria y Comercio, Dirección General de Estadística. *Revista de Estadística.* All volumes 1942–1963, México, D.F.

United Nations

United Nations. *Comparison of Steel Making Processes.* New York, 1962.
————. *European Steel Exports and Steel Demand in Non-European Countries.* Geneva, 1953.
————. *An Inquiry into the Iron and Steel Industry of Mexico.* New York, 1954.
————. *The Manufacture of Industrial Machinery in Latin America.* Vol. I, *Brazil.* New York, 1963.
————. *Possibilities of Integrated Industrial Development in Central America.* New York, 1964.

————. *Problems and Perspectives of Latin American Industrial Development.* Santiago: Comisió Económica para América Latina, 1963.

————. *Railways and Steel.* New York, 1960.

————. *Statistics of World Trade in Steel, 1961.* Geneva, 1963.

————. *Statistics of World Trade in Steel, 1913–1959.* Geneva, 1961.

————. *Statistical Yearbook.* New York: Statistical Office of the United Nations, various years.

————. *A Study of the Iron and Steel Industry in Latin America.* New York, 1957.

————. *Yearbook of International Trade Statistics.* New York: Statistical Office of the United Nations, 1953–1964.

Other

Inter-American Development Commission. *The Coal Fields and Iron Deposits of Mexico.* Washington, D.C., n.d.

International Cooperation Administration. *Operational Data, Small Steel Rolling Mill.* Washington, D.C., 1958.

International Monetary Fund. *Balance of Payments Yearbook.* Washington, D.C.

Organization of American States. *Economic and Social Survey of Latin America, 1961.* Washington, D.C.: Pan American Union, 1962.

Pan American Union. *Iron.* Washington, D.C., 1954.

United States Department of Commerce. *Industrial Scrap Generation: Iron and Steel, Copper, Aluminum.* Washington, D.C., 1957.

United States Tariff Commission. *Mining and Manufacturing Industries in Mexico.* Washington, D.C., 1946.

GENERAL PUBLICATIONS

Aceves Monteón, Adalberto. "Integración de la Industria Automovilista en México." Unpublished thesis, Universidad Nacional Autonoma de México, 1961.

Acosta Lagunos, Agustín. "Consideraciones sobre el Análisis Económico de Empresas." Unpublished thesis, Universidad Nacional Autonoma de México, 1964.

Altos Hornos de México, S.A. *Avante,* January, 1959, Monclova.

————. *Informe Anual, 1960.*

American Metal Market. *Metal Statistics 1963.* New York, 1964.

Antonio de Silva, José. "Problems of Utilizing Coal Resources in the Industrialization of Northern Mexico," *Basic Industries in Texas and Northern Mexico* (Latin American Studies IX). Austin: University of Texas Press, 1950).

Aramburu, Marcelo G. "Consumption of Iron and Steel Products in

Mexico," in United Nations, *A Study of the Iron and Steel Industry in Latin America*, p. 440.

———. "El Crecimiento de la Industria Siderúrgica en México," *Primero Congreso Nacional de la Industrial Siderúrgica*. México, D.F.: Imprenta Nuevo Mundo, 1956.

Bargallo, Modesto. *La Minería y la Metalurgía*. México, D.F.: Fondo de Cultura Económica, 1955.

Bernal Muñoz, Raul. *Fabricación de Muelles para Automóviles y Camiones*. México, D.F.: Banco de México, 1952.

Bernstein, Marvin D. "The Economic Organization of the Mexican Coal Industry," *Inter-American Economic Affairs*, Spring, 1952, pp. 73–91, Washington.

———. "The History and Economic Organization of the Mexican Mining Industry." Unpublished doctoral dissertation, The University of Texas, 1951.

Blair, Calvin P. "Nacional Financiera, Entrepreneurship in a Mixed Economy," in *Public Policy and Private Enterprise in Mexico*. Edited by Raymond Vernon. Cambridge, Massachusetts: Harvard University Press, 1964.

Blair, John M. *Price Discrimination in Steel*. Washington, D.C.: Government Printing Office, 1941.

Bullard, Freda. "Mexico's Natural Gas." 1964. To be published by Bureau of Business Research, The University of Texas.

Cámara Nacional de la Industria de Construcción. *Memoria del segundo Congreso Mexicano de la Industria de la Construcción*, Vol. II. México, D.F.: Talleres Lithograficos de la Espera, 1959.

Cámara Nacional de la Industria del Hierro y del Acero, *Comercio Exterior* (English edition).

———. *Glosario de Terminología Técnica Siderúrgica*. México, D.F., 1947.

———. *Circular No. 17, Nuevas Estadísticas de Importación de Productos Siderúrgicos*. México, D.F., September 14, 1964.

———. *Circular No. 18, Nuevas Estadísticas de Importación de "Manufacturas Metálicas."* México, D.F., September 21, 1964.

———. *Circular No. 19, Nuevas Estadísticas de Exportación de Productos Siderúrgicos*. México, D.F., September 28, 1964.

———. *Primer Congreso Nacional de la Industria Siderúrgica*. México, D.F.: Imprenta Neuvo Mundo, 1956.

———. *Segundo Congreso Nacional de la Industria Siderúrgica*. México, D.F.: Imprenta Nuevo Mundo, 1957.

———. *Tercer Congreso Nacional de la Industria Siderúrgica*. México, D.F.: Imprenta Nuevo Mundo, 1961.

Cámara Nacional de la Industria de Transformación. *Segundo Congreso*

Nacional de la Industria de Transformación: Memoria y Documentos. México, D.F.: Edición y Distribucion Ibero Americana de Publicaciones, S.A., 1953.

Castillo, Arturo del. *Tubería Soldada de Gran Diámetro.* México, D.F.: Banco de México, S.A. 1953.

Chase Manhattan Bank. "Iron and Steel in Latin America," *Mexican American Review,* March, 1957, pp. 36–45.

Checa de Codes, Juan Manuel. *La Industria Siderúrgica en Hispanoamérica.* Madrid: Artes Gráficas Ibarra, S.A., 1953.

Chutro, John Joseph. "The Dynamic Decade in the Industrial Growth of Mexico, 1939–1950." Unpublished master's thesis, The University of Texas, 1954.

Comisión de la Cuenca del Rio Tepacatepec. *Desarrollo de la Industria Siderúrgica en la Costa del Pacífico.* México, D.F., 1956.

Comisión Económica para América Latina. *Examen Preliminar de las Posibilidades de Desarrollo Industrial Integrado en Centroamérica.* Mar del Plata, Argentina, 1963.

Comité para Programación de la Industria Siderúrgica. *Programación del Desarrollo de la Industria Siderúrgica Mexicana.* México, D.F., 1962.

Compañía Fundidora de Fierro y Acero de Monterrey, S.A. (Price Book). Monterrey, 1912.

Constructora Nacional de Carros de Ferrocarril, S.A. *Furgones.* Mexico, D.F., 1959.

———. *Informe Anual, 1955.* México, D.F.: Talleres Gráficos de Impresiones Modernas, S.A., 1956.

Cortés Obregón, Salvador. "The Coal Used in the Mexican Iron and Steel Industry," in United Nations, *A Study of the Iron and Steel Industry in Latin America.* New York, 1954.

Dirección General de Estadística. *Compendio Estadístico 1960.* Mexico, 1962.

Economic Commission for Latin America. *Economic Bulletin for Latin America,* Vol. IV, No. 2. Santiago, 1959.

Electric Furnace Survey Group. *Comparative Economics of Open Hearth and Electric Furnace for Production of Low Carbon Steel.* Pittsburgh: Bituminous Coal Research, 1953.

Ferrocarriles Nacionales de México. *Necesidades de Carros de Ferrocarril, 1959–1964.* Monograph, n.d.

Finley, Moses I. *The World of Odysseus.* New York: Meridian Books, 1959.

Florence, P. Sargant. *Post-War Investment Location and Size of Plant.* London: Cambridge University Press. 1962.

"Food Canning Grows," *Mexican American Review.* October, 1950, pp. 13, 32–35. México, D.F.

Friedmann, Wolfgang, and G. Kalmanoff. *Joint International Business Ventures.* New York: Columbia University Press, 1961.

García Villarreal, Carlos. "El Mercado de Nacional Financiera y Finanzas Privadas." Unpublished thesis, Instituto Tecnológico de Monterrey, 1961.

Garza, Vargillo, Jr. "Brief Sketch of the Industrial Development of Monterrey," *Basic Industries in Texas and Northern Mexico.* Latin American Studies IX. Austin: University of Texas Press, 1950.

Glade, William Patton. "The Role of Government Enterprise in the Development of Underdeveloped Regions: Mexico, a Case Study." Unpublished doctoral dissertation, The University of Texas, 1955.

González L., Alejandro. "Un Estudio en la Cía. Fundidora de Fierro y Acero de Monterrey, S.A." Unpublished thesis, Universidad Nacional Autónoma de México, 1947.

González V., Fernando. "La Producción de Aceros Especiales en México." México, D.F.: Banco de México, S.A. Mimeographed. 1957.

González, Jenaro. *Riqueza Minera y Yacimientos Minerales de México.* México, D.F.: Banco de México, S.A., 1947.

Gordon, Wendell C. *The Economy of Latin America.* New York: Columbia University Press, 1953.

Gouvea de Bulhões, Octavio. *Función de los Precios en el Desarrollo.* México, D.F.: Centro de Estudios Monetarios Latinoamericanos, 1961.

Hartshorne, Richard. "Location Factors in the Iron and Steel Industry," *Economic Geography*, July, 1928. Concord, New Hampshire: Clark University.

Hernández Moreno, Jorge. "Ciudad Sahagún: Una Experiencia de Desarrollo en México." Unpublished thesis, Universidad Nacional Autonoma de México. 1961.

Hexner, Ervin. *The International Steel Cartel.* Chapel Hill: University of North Carolina Press, 1943.

Hirschman, Albert O. *The Strategy of Economic Development.* New Haven, Connecticut: Yale University Press, 1958.

Instituto de Investigaciones Económicas. *La Intervención del Estado en la Economia.* México, D.F.: Talleres de Baz Gráfica y Ediciones, S. de R.L., 1955.

Instituto Latinoamericano de Fierro y del Acero. *Reportorio de las Empresas Siderúrgicas.* Santiago: Imprentas Mueller, 1962.

———. *Análisis del Mercado de Tubos de Acero sin Costura en América Latina.* Santiago, 1962.

Izquierdo, Rafael. "Protectionism in Mexico," in *Public Policy and Private Enterprise in Mexico.* Edited by Raymond Vernon. Cambridge, Massachusetts: Harvard University Press, 1964.

Latapi, Andrés. "Concepto y Responsibilidades de la Gerencia," in

Tercer Congreso de la Industria Siderúrgica. México, D.F.: Imprenta Nuevo Mundo, 1961.

Marín González, Manuel. *Fabricación de Estufas Domesticas.* México, D.F.: Banco de México, S.A. 1953.

Martínez D., Guillermo. *Intentos de Control de Precios en México.* México, D.F.: Talleres de Secretaría de Educación Pública, 1950.

Martirena de Mantel, Ana M. "Integración y Economías de Escala," in *El Trimestre Económico.* México, D.F.: Fondo de Cultura Económica.

"Mexico's Steel Industry: A Race with the Future," *Mexican American Review,* June, 1962, México, D.F.

Navarette, Crispin. *La Producción de Acero Eléctrico en México.* México, D.F.: Banco de México, S.A., n.d.

Negocios, July, 1964, México, D.F.

Palacio, Arturo. *Fabricación de Productos de Hojalata.* México, D.F.: Banco de México, S.A., n.d.

Pape, H. R. "Five Years of Achievement at Altos Hornos Steel Company," in *Basic Industries in Texas and Northern Mexico* (Latin American Studies IX). Austin: University of Texas Press, 1950.

Peña, Joaquin de la. *La Industria Siderúrgica en Mexico.* Mexico, D.F.: Edición y Distribución Ibero Americana de Publicaciones, S.A., 1951.

Pérez Molina, Federico. "La Industria Siderúrgica en la América Latina." Unpublished thesis, Universidad Nacional Autónoma de México, 1963.

Pounds, Norman G. *Geography of Iron and Steel.* London: Hutchinson University Library, 1939.

Prebisch, Raúl, "Panorama y Perspectivas de la Industria Siderúrgica en América Latina," *Comercio Exterior,* January, 1960, pp. 20–23.

Prieto, Carlos. "La Industria Siderúrgica," *México, 50 Años de Revolución,* I: *La Economía.* México, D.F.: Fondo de Cultura Económica, 1960.

————. *Tres Industrias Mexicanas antes la ALAC.* México, D.F.: Colección SELA, 1962.

Ramírez, Ramón. *Tendencias de la Economía Mexicana.* Published thesis, Universidad Nacional Autónoma de México, 1962.

Realme Rodríguez, Oscar. "La Industria Siderúrgica Nacional." Unpublished thesis, Universidad Nacional Autónoma de México, 1946.

Rivera Rangel, Carlos A. "La Siderúrgica y la Integración Industrial de México." Unpublished thesis, Universidad Nacional Autónoma de México, 1962.

Robles, Gonzalo. "La Industria Siderúrgica en México," *Comercio Exterior,* Vol. VI, No. 5, pp. 214–218, México, D.F.

Sada, Pablo. "Some Notes on the Organization of the Monclova Steel

Works," in United Nations, *A Study of the Iron and Steel Industry in Latin America.* New York, 1954.

Salcido Morineau, Arturo. "El Mercado del Acero en México." Unpublished thesis. Universidad Nacional Autónoma de México, 1964.

Salinas Lozano, Raúl. *La Intervención del Estado y la Cuestión de los Precios.* México, D.F.: Editorial América, 1944.

Sánchez Hurtado, Carlos. *Evolución Histórica de la Industria Siderúrgica Chileno e Ibero-Americana.* Santiago: Editorial Nacimiento, 1952.

Schubert, H. R. *History of the British Iron and Steel Industry.* London: Routledge and Kegan Paul, 1957.

Torón Villegas, Luis. *Estudio de los Yacimientos Ferríferos de México.* Vol. II. México, D.F.: Banco de México, S.A., 1945.

―――. *La Industria Siderúrgica Pesada del Norte de México.* México, D.F.: Banco de México, S.A., 1963.

Torre Kuhn, Eduardo de la. *El Mercado Nacional de Carros de Ferrocarril.* Published thesis, Universidad Nacional Autónoma de México, 1962.

Truett, Dale B. "The Development of the Transport Equipment Industry in Mexico." Unpublished master's thesis, The University of Texas, 1964.

Tubos de Acero de México. *Informe Anual de 1963.* Veracruz, 1964.

Villarreal, Arnulfo. *El Carbón Mineral en México.* México, D.F.: Edición y Distribución Ibero Americano de Publicaciones, S.A., 1954.

Watkins, Ralph W. *The Market for Steel in Mexico.* New York: Frederick A. Praeger, 1964.

Wythe, George. *Industry in Latin America.* Boulder: University of Colorado Press, 1945.

Zimmermann, Erich. *World Resources and Industries.* New York: Harper and Brothers, 1951.

Index